BIO 2010

Transforming Undergraduate Education

for Future Research Biologists

Committee on Undergraduate Biology Education to Prepare
Research Scientists for the 21st Century

Board on Life Sciences
Division on Earth and Life Studies

NATIONAL RESEARCH COUNCIL
OF THE NATIONAL ACADEMIES

THE NATIONAL ACADEMIES PRESS
Washington, D.C.
www.nap.edu

THE NATIONAL ACADEMIES PRESS   500 Fifth Street, N.W.   Washington, DC 20001

NOTICE: The project that is the subject of this report was approved by the Governing Board of the National Research Council, whose members are drawn from the councils of the National Academy of Sciences, the National Academy of Engineering, and the Institute of Medicine. The members of the committee responsible for the report were chosen for their special competences and with regard for appropriate balance.

This study was supported by Contract Number N01-OD-4-2139, Task Order 64 between the National Academies and the National Institutes of Health and Award Number 71200-500115 between the National Academies and the Howard Hughes Medical Institute. Any opinions, findings, conclusions, or recommendations expressed in this publication are those of the author(s) and do not necessarily reflect the views of the organizations or agencies that provided support for the project.

Library of Congress Cataloging-in-Publication Data

Bio2010 : transforming undergraduate education for future research biologists / Committee on Undergraduate Biology Education to Prepare Research Scientists for the 21st Century, Board on Life Sciences, Division on Earth and Life Studies, the National Research Council of the National Academies.
    p. cm.
Includes bibliographical references and index.
  ISBN 0-309-08535-7 (pbk.)
  1. Biology—Study and teaching (Higher)—United States. I. National Research Council (U.S.). Committee on Undergraduate Biology Education to Prepare Research Scientists for the 21st Century.
  QH319.A1 B56 2002
  570'.71'173—dc21
                    2002152267

Additional copies of this report are available from the National Academies Press, 500 Fifth Street, N.W., Lockbox 285, Washington, DC 20055; (800) 624-6242 or (202) 334-3313 (in the Washington metropolitan area); Internet, http://www.nap.edu

First Printing, January 2003
Second Printing, August 2003

THE NATIONAL ACADEMIES
Advisers to the Nation on Science, Engineering, and Medicine

The **National Academy of Sciences** is a private, nonprofit, self-perpetuating society of distinguished scholars engaged in scientific and engineering research, dedicated to the furtherance of science and technology and to their use for the general welfare. Upon the authority of the charter granted to it by the Congress in 1863, the Academy has a mandate that requires it to advise the federal government on scientific and technical matters. Dr. Bruce M. Alberts is president of the National Academy of Sciences.

The **National Academy of Engineering** was established in 1964, under the charter of the National Academy of Sciences, as a parallel organization of outstanding engineers. It is autonomous in its administration and in the selection of its members, sharing with the National Academy of Sciences the responsibility for advising the federal government. The National Academy of Engineering also sponsors engineering programs aimed at meeting national needs, encourages education and research, and recognizes the superior achievements of engineers. Dr. Wm. A. Wulf is president of the National Academy of Engineering.

The **Institute of Medicine** was established in 1970 by the National Academy of Sciences to secure the services of eminent members of appropriate professions in the examination of policy matters pertaining to the health of the public. The Institute acts under the responsibility given to the National Academy of Sciences by its congressional charter to be an adviser to the federal government and, upon its own initiative, to identify issues of medical care, research, and education. Dr. Harvey V. Fineberg is president of the Institute of Medicine.

The **National Research Council** was organized by the National Academy of Sciences in 1916 to associate the broad community of science and technology with the Academy's purposes of furthering knowledge and advising the federal government. Functioning in accordance with general policies determined by the Academy, the Council has become the principal operating agency of both the National Academy of Sciences and the National Academy of Engineering in providing services to the government, the public, and the scientific and engineering communities. The Council is administered jointly by both Academies and the Institute of Medicine. Dr. Bruce M. Alberts and Dr. Wm. A. Wulf are chair and vice chair, respectively, of the National Research Council.

www.national-academies.org

Foreword

This report continues the National Academies' efforts in the reform of education by calling on researchers to recognize the importance of teaching and to join together with educators to promote undergraduate learning. The goal in this case is to prepare the next generation of biological researchers for the tremendous opportunities ahead. Attaining this goal will require that faculty spend more time discussing their teaching with their colleagues, both within and outside of their own field or department. The enthusiastic participation of the Bio2010 committee members in this study demonstrates how deeply our leading researchers value education. It also proves that chemists, physicists, mathematicians, and biologists can learn from each other, as well as from talented educators. As the report makes clear, biological research today has reached a very exciting stage, and many more biological scientists with strong backgrounds in physics and chemistry will be needed. Moreover, collaborations between established scientists who were trained in different disciplines will be facilitated if they learn to communicate with its practitioners at an early stage in their careers and appreciate the contributions that each discipline can make to biology.

Undergraduate education is a crucial link in the preparation of future researchers. Many university faculty care deeply about education, but most of them have received no training in how to teach. This report offers many suggestions for faculty who would like to improve their teaching. It presents examples of what others have done and resources for further investigation. It also calls on colleges, universities, and others to provide support for faculty who want to devote energy to improving teaching and to producing new teaching materials.

The National Academies have produced dozens of reports on education in recent years. Many of these reports are useful resources for college faculty. *Science Teaching Reconsidered* is a handbook for faculty to help them improve their teaching. *Transforming Undergraduate Education in Science, Mathematics, Engineering and Technology* promotes a vision in which these subjects would become accessible to all students. *How People Learn* and *Inquiry and the National Science Education Standards* are written for precollege faculty, but they contain important ideas for everyone on how knowledge of cognitive science can inform teaching and learning. All of these resources are freely available on our Web site at *www.national academies.org*.

Publishing reports is not enough. As a result of ideas presented in this Bio2010 report, the National Academies will launch a pilot program, a Summer Institute for Undergraduate Biology Education. The Institute will bring teams of faculty from research universities together to present them with proven ways to improve student learning, as well as to allow them to share their own expertise concerning effective undergraduate teaching.

In closing, I would like to thank Lubert Stryer for his inspired, energetic leadership of this important project, as well as the members of the committee and its staff for each of their critical contributions. They have served the nation well.

Bruce Alberts
President, National Academy of Sciences
Chair, National Research Council

Preface

Increasingly, biomedical researchers must be comfortable applying diverse aspects of mathematics and the physical sciences to their pursuit of biological knowledge. Biomedical researchers advance society's understanding of many topics, not just human disease. They work with diverse model organisms and study behavior in systems ranging from the molecular to the organismal using traditional biological techniques as well as high-tech approaches. Undergraduate biology students who become comfortable with the ideas of mathematics and physical sciences from the start of their education will be better positioned to contribute to future discoveries in biomedical research. For this reason the National Institutes of Health and the Howard Hughes Medical Institute asked the National Research Council to evaluate the undergraduate education of this particular group of students. The committee began its work in the fall of 2000.

The report recommends a comprehensive reevaluation of undergraduate science education for future biomedical researchers. In particular it calls for a renewed discussion on the ways that engineering and computer science, as well as chemistry, physics, and mathematics are presented to life science students. The conclusions of the report are based on input from chemists, physicists, and mathematicians, not just practicing research biologists. The committee recognizes that all undergraduate science education is interconnected. Changes cannot be made solely to benefit future biomedical researchers. The impact on undergraduates studying other types of biology, as well as other sciences, cannot be ignored as reforms are considered. The Bio2010 report therefore provides ideas and options suitable for various academic situations and diverse types of institutions. It is hoped that the reader will use these possibilities to initiate discussions on the goals and methods of teaching used within their own department, institution, or professional society.

This report is the product of many individuals. The committee would like to thank those who participated in the Panel on Chemistry, the Panel on Physics and Engineering, the Panel on Mathematics and Computer Science, and the Workshop on Innovative Undergraduate Biology Education. The names of all these individuals are listed in the appendices of this report. Their input played an essential role in the committee's deliberations.

This report has been reviewed in draft form by individuals chosen for their diverse perspectives and technical expertise, in accordance with procedures approved by the NRC's Report Review Committee. The purpose of this independent review is to provide candid and critical comments that will assist the institution in making its published report as sound as possible and to ensure that the report meets institutional standards for objectivity, evidence, and responsiveness to the study charge. The review comments and draft manuscript remain confidential to protect the integrity of the deliberative process. We wish to thank the following individuals for their review of this report:

> Norma Allewell, University of Maryland, College Park
> Wyatt Anderson, University of Georgia
> Michael Antolin, Colorado State University
> Susan Chaplin, University of St. Thomas
> Joan Ferrini-Mundy, Michigan State University
> Ronald Henry, Georgia State University
> Nancy Stewart Mills, Trinity University
> Jeanne Narum, Project Kaleidoscope
> Paul Sternberg, California Institute of Technology

Although the reviewers listed above have provided constructive comments and suggestions, they were not asked to endorse the conclusions or recommendations nor did they see the final draft of the report before its release. The review of this report was overseen by William B. Wood of the University of Colorado and May R. Berenbaum of the University of Illinois. Appointed by the National Research Council, they were responsible for making certain that an independent examination of this report was carried out in accordance with institutional procedures and that all review comments were carefully considered. Responsibility for the final content of this report rests entirely with the authoring committee and the institution.

Contents

Executive Summary

The interplay of the recombinant DNA, instrumentation, and digital revolutions has profoundly transformed biological research. The confluence of these three innovations has led to important discoveries, such as the mapping of the human genome. How biologists design, perform, and analyze experiments is changing swiftly. Biological concepts and models are becoming more quantitative, and biological research has become critically dependent on concepts and methods drawn from other scientific disciplines. The connections between the biological sciences and the physical sciences, mathematics, and computer science are rapidly becoming deeper and more extensive. The ways that scientists communicate, interact, and collaborate are undergoing equally rapid and dramatic transformations, which are driven by the accessibility of vast computing power and facile information exchange over the Internet.

In contrast to biological research, undergraduate biology education has changed relatively little during the past two decades. The ways in which most future research biologists are educated are geared to the biology of the past, rather than to the biology of the present or future. Like research in the life sciences, undergraduate education must be transformed to prepare students effectively for the biology that lies ahead. Life sciences majors must acquire a much stronger foundation in the physical sciences (chemistry and physics) and mathematics than they now get. Connections between biology and the other scientific disciplines need to be developed and reinforced so that interdisciplinary thinking and work become second nature. Connections within biology are equally important and the relevance of fields such as population biology, plant biology, and cognitive science to biomedical research should not be ignored. Equally important, teaching and learning must be made more active to engage undergraduates, fully prepare them for graduate study, and give them an enduring sense of the power and beauty of creative inquiry. In light of these realities, this report describes changes in undergraduate education designed to improve the preparation of students in the life sciences, with a particular emphasis on the education that will be needed in the future for careers in biomedical research.

THE REPORT

This study was conducted at the initiative of its sponsors, the National Institutes of Health (NIH) and the Howard Hughes Medical Institute (HHMI). Both sponsors support numerous diverse projects in biomedical research. They view future research as increasingly interdisciplinary and believe that exposing today's undergraduates to a more interdisciplinary curriculum will help them to better collaborate with their scientific peers in other disciplines as well as to design more interdisciplinary projects on their own. The National Research Council (NRC) convened the Committee on Undergraduate Biology Education to Prepare Research Scientists for the 21st Century to prepare a report addressing issues related to undergraduate education of future biomedical researchers. The committee was charged with examining the formal undergraduate education, training, and experience required to prepare the next generation of life science majors, with a particular emphasis on the preparation of students for careers in biomedical research. One goal of the project was to identify the basic skills and concepts of mathematics, chemistry, physics, computer science, and engineering that can assist students in making novel interdisciplinary connections. The complete formal charge to the committee can be found in Appendix A.

CONCLUSIONS

To successfully undertake careers in research after graduation, students will need scientific knowledge, practice with experimental design, quantitative abilities, and communication skills. While this study was conducted to consider what is appropriate for the education of future biomedical researchers, the committee recognizes that students with many other career goals will take the same courses and believes that many of the ideas for increasing the interdisciplinary nature of coursework would be equally beneficial for all students. Colleges and universities should reexamine current curricula in light of changing practices in biological research. In addition, faculty should attempt to utilize teaching approaches that are most likely to help students learn these skills. For example, independent or group projects (both library- and laboratory-based) are likely to help foster a sense of ownership by students, which may in turn encourage them to take the initiative to investigate a topic in detail. Presenting examples of current research to show that science consists of unanswered questions will also intrigue and inspire more students to probe problems in depth. It is important for these efforts to start at the very beginning of a student's education in the K-12 years, and for them to be continued and enhanced in the first year of college. (Some ideas for providing this exposure to high school students can be found in a recent NRC report on advanced placement and international baccalaureate courses [NRC, 2002] and in an earlier NRC report, *Transforming Undergraduate Education in Science, Mathematics, Engineering, and Technology* [NRC, 1999b].) Offering exciting introductory courses will help attract more students to enroll in biology courses, increasing the number who might consider biomedical research as a career. Increasing the number of students who consider biology as a major may increase the quality of future biomedical researchers.

Courses

Many science and mathematics courses are taught as sets of facts, rather than by explaining how the material was discovered or developed over time. Covering the history of the field, demonstrating the process of discovery, or presenting other stories as examples of how scientists work—while clearly illustrating why the knowledge that has been gained is relevant to the lives and surroundings of the students—is an excellent way to engage undergraduates. The committee believes that success of a future biomedical researcher requires not just expertise in the specific biological system under study, but a conceptual understanding of the science of life and where a specific research topic fits into the overall picture. Teaching undergraduates about the many different ways in which biologists approach research, including lab work, fieldwork, and computer modeling, will help them to understand the unifying themes that tie together the diverse kinds of life on earth. Much of today's biomedical research is at the interface between biology and the physical, mathematical, or information sciences. Most colleges and universities already require their biology majors to enroll in courses in mathematics and physical science. However, faculty often do not integrate these subjects into the biology courses they teach. This can result in students with a shortsighted view of the connections between all the scientific disciplines involved in the study of the biological world, and produce students who do not see the relevance of their other science courses to their chosen field of study.

Laboratory Experience

Independent work, both inside and outside the classroom, is a wonderful way to expose students to the world of science. Class projects can provide opportunities for students to analyze original data, experience teamwork, and practice scientific writing and presentation skills. Independent research gives students a real world view of life as a researcher. Colleges and universities should provide all students with opportunities to become engaged in research, whether that be in an on-campus independent research experience with faculty; an internship at nearby institutions (biotechnology or pharmaceutical companies, national laboratories, government agencies, independent research centers, or other academic institutions); or through an extended research-based project in a course and/or laboratory.

Quantitative Skills

The lack of a quantitative viewpoint in biology courses can result in students who are mathematically talented losing interest in studying the life sciences. While not all students who pursue an education in the biomedical sciences have an equal interest or predilection for mathematics, it is important that all students understand the growing relevance of quantitative science in addressing life-science questions. Thus, a better integration of quantitative applications in biology would not only enhance life science education for all students, but also decrease the chances that mathematically talented students would reject life sciences as too soft. Similar consideration must be given to the integration of physics and chemistry into a life science curriculum. In biomedical research today, complex questions are usually addressed by teams of scientists that bring different perspectives and insights to the issues being studied. Many of today's top biomedical researchers came to their work after undergraduate or graduate education in another field, most notably physics and/or chemistry. However, there is often a profound communication barrier between these researchers and those educated as biologists. Increasing the amount of mathematics and of physical and information sciences taught to new biology students, and the opportunity for physical science majors to take courses with biological content, would improve the possibilities for productive collaborations.

Mathematics teaching presents a special case. Most biology majors take no more than one year of calculus, although some also take an additional semester of statistics. Very few are exposed to discrete mathematics, linear algebra, probability, and modeling topics, which could greatly enhance their future research careers. These are often considered advanced courses; however, many aspects of discrete math or linear algebra that would be relevant to biology students do not require calculus as a prerequisite. While calculus remains an important topic for future biologists, the committee does not believe biology students should study calculus to the exclusion of other types of mathematics. Newly designed courses in mathematics that cover some calculus as well as the other types of math mentioned above would be suitable for biology majors and would also prove useful to students enrolled in many other undergraduate majors.

Role of Medical School Requirements

Another special issue is the impact of medical school admissions requirements on undergraduate biology curricula. The committee did not specifically address the needs of premedical students in making its recommendations. However, the committee recognizes that specific courses are currently required for medical school admission and that the need to prepare students for the Medical College Admissions Test (MCAT) constrains course offerings and content at most institutions. Departments of physics, chemistry, and mathematics, as well as departments of biology, feel pressure to cover the material tested on the MCAT in their introductory courses to the exclusion of other potential topics.

Implementation

Incorporating mathematics, physical science, and emerging fields such as the information sciences into a biology curriculum is not easy, especially for faculty who do not consider themselves well versed in those topics. One way to start is to add modules into existing biology courses. Throughout this report, modules are mentioned as a way to modify courses without completely revamping the syllabus. The committee uses the word "module" to mean a self-contained set of material on a specific topic that could be inserted into various different types of preexisting courses. For example, modules can provide opportunities to add quantitative examples or experimental data to a course. The modules would demonstrate the necessity of using mathematics and physical and information sciences to solve biological problems. Administrators, funding agencies, and professional societies should all work to encourage the collaboration of faculty in different departments and the development of teaching materials, including modules of the type mentioned above, that incorporate mathematics, physical science, or information science into the teaching of biology. The creation of new teaching materials is a significant undertaking. It will require a major commitment from college and university administrators and funders to be successful. Faculty must feel encouraged to spend the time necessary to dedicate themselves to the task of understanding the integrative relationships of biology, mathematics, and the physical sciences, and how they can be combined into either existing courses or new courses. In addition, faculty development opportunities must be provided so that faculty can learn from each other and from experts in education about the best approaches for facilitating student learning.

The following box presents a summary of the most important recommendations in this report. Throughout the text of the report, other recommendations are made and other ideas are presented. Not all of the ideas presented here are proven approaches. In any new educational effort it is important to define goals and create an assessment plan to determine if the student learning goals are being met. The committee believes that the general recommendations presented here are appropriate for all institutions, while recognizing that not all institutions will use the same mechanisms to achieve these goals. The specific mechanisms appropriate for each individual institution of higher education will depend on the skills and interests of both their students and their faculty. This report presents numerous ideas in the belief that each institution will identify for itself the most relevant options. The recommendations that follow are directed at the next generation of life science majors, particularly those preparing for careers in biomedical research.

The ideas presented here for transforming the undergraduate education of life science majors are demanding, but the committee believes that significant change is realizable within this decade if these recommendations are acted upon. Reform will require concerted action by faculty, administrators, professional societies and other educational organizations, foundations, industry, and government. The process begins with faculty and administrators. The committee urges each academic institution to critically review how it educates its future biologists. Departmental retreats are a good setting for an initial examination of current educational objectives, practices, and outcomes. The circle should eventually be broadened by inviting faculty from different departments to come together with administrators and discuss aspirations and goals for the coming decade. The resources needed to effect these changes must be clearly defined and a realistic path must be charted to complete the planning stage. University administrators will need to actively support faculty development and remove barriers to interdisciplinary teaching, a key aspect of enhancing undergraduate education. Departments and colleges must find new ways to help individual faculty and academic departments innovate and reward their efforts in creating, assessing, and sustaining new educational programs. For example, faculty interested in adapting teaching approaches for their own use or in creating new teaching materials should have lighter than normal requirements for teaching, research, or service while actively engaged in such projects. Also, travel funds earmarked especially for faculty development or education meetings should be provided to enable faculty to participate in meetings that enhance their teaching capabilities. These funds must be targeted toward faculty who are specifically seeking to build and sustain high-quality programs that can be assessed and demonstrated as effective.

Many professional societies already play important roles in furthering innovation and promoting higher educational standards. They can play a heightened role in the future by actively promoting the importance of undergraduate education and faculty development, as well as continuing to serve as a meeting ground for the sharing of educational programs, technologies, and teaching materials. They can also aid the process by finding ways to highlight and publish creative educational endeavors and accomplishments through society-specific channels much in the same way that they highlight and publish new research. Annual summer workshops on undergraduate biology education would also be an effective means to evaluate educational innovation and identify best practices; further faculty development; and create new modules, books, laboratory guides, and other materials needed to effect the changes recommended in this report.

Recommendations

1. Given the profound changes in the nature of biology and how biological research is performed and communicated, each institution of higher education should reexamine its current courses and teaching approaches to see if they meet the needs of today's undergraduate biology students. Those selecting the new approaches should consider the importance of building a strong foundation in mathematics and the physical and information sciences to prepare students for research that is increasingly interdisciplinary in character. The implementation of new approaches should be accompanied by a parallel process of assessment, to verify that progress is being made toward the institutional goal of student learning. Lists of relevant concepts are provided within the body of this report. (pages 27, 32, 34, 37, 38, and 41)

2. Concepts, examples, and techniques from mathematics, and the physical and information sciences should be included in biology courses, and biological concepts and examples should be included in other science courses. Faculty in biology, mathematics, and physical sciences must work collaboratively to find ways of integrating mathematics and physical sciences into life science courses as well as providing avenues for incorporating life science examples that reflect the emerging nature of the discipline into courses taught in mathematics and physical sciences. (page 47)

3. Successful interdisciplinary teaching will require new materials and approaches. College and university administrators, as well as funding agencies, should support mathematics and science faculty in the development or adaptation of techniques that improve interdisciplinary education for biologists. These techniques would include courses, modules (on biological problems suitable for study in mathematics and physical science courses and vice versa), and other teaching materials. These endeavors are time-consuming and difficult and will require serious financial support. In addition,

for truly interdisciplinary education to be achieved, administrative and financial barriers to cross-departmental collaboration between faculty must be eliminated. (page 60)

4. Laboratory courses should be as interdisciplinary as possible, since laboratory experiments confront students with real-world observations do not separate well into conventional disciplines. (page 75)

5. All students should be encouraged to pursue independent research as early as is practical in their education. They should be able to receive academic credit for independent research done in collaboration with faculty or with off-campus researchers. (page 87)

6. Seminar-type courses that highlight cutting-edge developments in biology should be provided on a continual and regular basis throughout the four-year undergraduate education of students. Communicating the excitement of biological research is crucial to attracting, retaining, and sustaining a greater diversity of students to the field. These courses would combine presentations by faculty with student projects on research topics. (page 91)

7. Medical school admissions requirements and the Medical College Admissions Test (MCAT) are hindering change in the undergraduate biology curriculum and should be reexamined in light of the recommendations in this report. (page 111)

8. Faculty development is a crucial component to improving undergraduate biology education. Efforts must be made on individual campuses and nationally to provide faculty the time necessary to refine their own understanding of how the integrative relationships of biology, mathematics, and the physical sciences can be best melded into either existing courses or new courses in the particular areas of science in which they teach. (page 113)

1

Introduction

MAJOR CHANGES IN RESEARCH COMPEL MAJOR CHANGES IN UNDERGRADUATE EDUCATION

The ways in which we think about and pursue research in biology[1] are changing rapidly. In the past decade, powerful innovations—including recombinant DNA, instrumentation, and the digital revolution—have altered fundamentally the ways in which biology is done. Biologists are increasingly intrigued by the challenges of deciphering how components such as molecules, cells, or organisms interact to produce higher-order structures and properties. They are studying the ways in which molecules can affect cells, or ways in which cells can affect organ systems, or how individual organisms affect populations and ecosystems. At all levels of biological organization, the elucidation and understanding of integrated systems are moving to center stage.

The elucidation of the sequence of the human genome is one of the remarkable fruits of this confluence. Knowledge of diverse genomes, from bacteria to worms to flies to humans, is revealing recurring motifs and mechanisms, and strengthening an appreciation for the fundamental unity of life. Biological concepts, models, and theories are becoming more quan-

---

[1]Throughout this report the terms biology and life sciences are used interchangeably to reflect this large family of disciplines and subdisciplines.

titative, and the connections between the life and physical sciences are becoming deeper and stronger. As a result, the predictive power of biology is also increasing swiftly.

How biological research is carried out is changing rapidly, too. Biologists increasingly do their work using sophisticated instrumentation that is rooted in the physical sciences. For example, synchrotron x-ray sources are used to determine three-dimensional structures of proteins. Focused laser beams allow manipulations of single molecules. Functional magnetic resonance imagers map activated regions of the brain. Highly parallel data acquisition, such as the use of simultaneous measurement of the expression levels of tens of thousands of genes in DNA arrays, has become commonplace. Computers now play a central role in the acquisition, storage, analysis, interpretation, and visualization of vast quantities of biological data.

Modern biology is becoming more dependent on the physical sciences (chemistry and physics) and engineering in multiple ways. First, as the analysis of biological systems advances at the cellular and molecular levels, the distinction between the physical and biological sciences blurs, and essential biological processes are most fruitfully treated in terms of their physical properties. Second, as biologists deal with systems at a higher level of complexity, theoretical tools from other fields increasingly are required to deal with the many simultaneously interacting components of such complex systems. For example, exocytosis and endocytosis are basic processes common to all cells; they are ultimately understood in terms of the physical chemistry of membrane fusion and fission. Another pertinent example is the study of genetic networks responsible for developmental processes. Here many genes interact combinatorially in positive and negative regulatory pathways to generate the spatial and temporal patterns exhibited in the adult organism. Understanding development requires theories of how these patterns form; physics, mathematics, and engineering provide advanced tools for formulating and testing such theories.

The ways in which scientists communicate and interact are undergoing equally rapid and dramatic transformations. Data and software are shared extensively over the Internet. Different kinds of data (e.g., genes with the corresponding diseases in the database Online Mendelian Inheritance in Man, available at *http://www.ncbi.nlm.nih.gov/omim*) are becoming linked. Investigators throughout the world query vast databases (e.g., Genbank, available at *http://www.ncbi.nlm.nih.gov/Genbank/Genbank Overview.html*) daily to design and interpret experiments. Many laboratories host highly informative Web sites, which complement their published papers. Investigators collaborate easily over large distances thanks to the Internet. Some of the most important problems in biology (e.g., the Human Genome Project) are now being tackled by dispersed teams of investigators working in concert. New kinds of scientific communities are emerging.

EVIDENCE THAT INTERDISCIPLINARY EDUCATION IS NECESSARY

The recent report entitled *The Role of the Private Sector in Training the Next Generation of Biomedical Scientists* concludes "In the postgenomic era of research, multidisciplinary and interdisciplinary research will command center stage, requiring team approaches and the collaboration of many individuals from vastly different fields, ranging from computational mathematics to clinical science" (American Cancer Society et al., 2000). The same report also states "The changing paradigm of research calls for innovations and changes in the education of scientists along the spectrum of K-12, undergraduate and graduate education." This is one of many calls to improve interdisciplinary education. A recent NRC report, *Addressing the Nation's Changing Needs for Biomedical and Behavioral Scientists*, recommends, "The NIH should expand its emphasis on multidisciplinary training in the basic biomedical sciences" (NRC, 2000a).

Numerous studies and workshops have addressed the growing research at the intersection of biology with other disciplines, further supporting the need for more interdisciplinary education. The NRC study *Strengthening the Linkages Between the Sciences and Mathematical Sciences* was published in 2000 (NRC, 2000c) and the report *Frontiers at the Interface of Computing and Biology* is nearing completion (NRC, unpublished report, 2002). The NRC has held workshops on interdisciplinary topics, including "Workshop on the Interface of Engineering and Biology: Catalyzing the Future; Bioinformatics: Converting Data to Knowledge." "Dynamical Modeling of Complex Biomedical Systems" was convened by the Board on Mathematical Sciences in 2001. Other recent NRC studies illustrate the wide-ranging applications of biology.[2]

---

[2]They include *A Strategy for Research in Space Biology and Medicine into the Next Century* (NRC, 1998); *Cells and Surveys: Should Biological Measures Be Included in Social Science Research?* (NRC, 2001a); *Health and Behavior: The Interplay of Biological, Behavioral, and*

Already, multidisciplinary projects are emphasized in solicitations for research grants. The National Science Foundation (NSF) and NIH work together on joint initiatives to support collaborative research in several areas, including computational neuroscience and research in mathematics and statistics related to mathematical biology research (National Institute of General Medical Sciences and National Science Foundation, *http:// www.nsf.gov/pubs/2002/nsf02125/nsf02125.htm*). The National Institute of General Medical Sciences has several initiatives to promote quantitative, interdisciplinary approaches to problems of biomedical significance, particularly those that involve the complex, interactive behavior of many components. For example, the Protein Structure Initiative supports the creation of partnerships such as the Berkeley Structural Genomics Center, run by Lawrence Berkeley National Laboratory in partnership with the University of California at Berkeley, Stanford University, and the University of North Carolina, Chapel Hill. Another initiative, the Biomedical Information Science and Technology Initiative, is at an earlier stage of development, but was set up to encourage the optimal use of computer science and technology to address problems in biology and medicine. The National Institute on Drug Abuse (NIDA) has supplemental funds available for principal investigators who want to develop and incorporate computational and theoretical modeling approaches into existing research projects. NIDA-funded researchers studying behavioral, cognitive, and neurobiological processes, and cellular and molecular mechanisms of drug abuse and addiction, are eligible for this supplemental funding. It is anticipated that funds will be used to bring state-of-the-art computational and theoretical modeling approaches to the analysis of ongoing research projects. In 2000, NIH established the National Institute of Biomedical Imaging and Bioengineering, which, among other activities, works with other institutes to provide funding under a Bioengineering Research Partnership program. This interdisciplinary focus is not limited to biology in the biomedical realm; for example, the NSF initiative BioComplexity in the Environment is designed for large teams with members who come from different disciplines as well as different institutions.

To successfully participate in the interdisciplinary research of the fu-

---

Societal Influences (NRC, 2001b); *The Aging Mind: Opportunities in Cognitive Research* (NRC, 2000d); and *From Monsoons to Microbes: Understanding the Ocean's Role in Human Health* (NRC, 2000c).

ture, biomedical scientists must be well versed in scientific topics beyond the range of traditional biology. Beginning exposure to these topics early is one key to educating biomedical researchers who deal easily with interdisciplinary research projects. Some graduate students are currently studying in this way, but many are not. Interdisciplinary education is even less common at the undergraduate level. For graduate students in biology, funding is most frequently provided by NIH, NSF, or HHMI. However, few fellowships are targeted for interdisciplinary graduate study. NSF developed the Integrative Graduate Education and Research Traineeship (IGERT) program to meet the challenges of preparing Ph.D. scientists and engineers with the "multidisciplinary backgrounds and the technical, professional, and personal skills needed for the career demands of the future" (National Science Foundation, 2000). The Whitaker Foundation offers Graduate Fellowships in Biomedical Engineering and has also provided funding to stimulate the creation of new departments or programs in biomedical engineering throughout the country. The Burroughs Wellcome Foundation offers Bridging Support for Physical/Computational Scientists Entering Biology and, in the past, supported a program for universities called Institutional Awards at the Scientific Interface that funded the development of interdisciplinary training programs for graduate and postdoctoral students.

RESEARCH ON EDUCATION CAN BENEFIT THE TEACHING OF UNDERGRADUATE BIOLOGY

The ways in which students are taught and learn biology are as important as the content of the material covered. The large lecture courses that are still the usual format for lower-division science classes often fail to keep the attention of some students. Recent research in education has validated several important insights into optimal conditions for student learning, as summarized, for example, in the NRC Report *How People Learn: Brain, Mind, Experience, and School* (NRC, 1999a). The report was written by a committee that included cognitive scientists, psychologists, and experts in research on education. The key findings of *How People Learn* were that:

1. Students come to the classroom with preconceptions about how the world works. If their initial understanding is not engaged, they may fail to grasp the new concepts and information that are taught, or they may learn them for the purposes of a test but revert to their preconceptions outside the classroom.

2. To develop confidence in an area of inquiry, students must (a) have a deep

foundation of factual knowledge, (b) understand facts and ideas in the context of a conceptual framework, and (c) organize knowledge in ways that facilitate retrieval and application.

3. A "metacognitive"[3] approach to instruction can help students learn to take control of their own learning by defining learning goals and monitoring their progress in achieving them.

One chapter of *How People Learn* describes how experts differ from novices. For example, it compares the different approaches to problem solving typically seen in a physicist and an undergraduate studying introductory physics. When asked to sort a pile of index cards containing questions, the physicists organized the cards based on concepts (such as Newton's second law) that would be used to determine the solution to the problem. The beginning student more often sorted the cards based on the objects involved in the problem (such as a spring or an inclined plane) (NRC, 1999a).

These insights in turn have become the basis for widespread efforts to reform the way that science in particular is taught, from elementary school through college. For the undergraduate level, in 1977 the NRC published a useful and practical handbook on teaching undergraduate science, *Science Teaching Reconsidered* (NRC, 1997b). It explains how student misconceptions can interfere with learning, how to evaluate teaching (assessment) and learning (exams), and how to choose instructional material. Numerous other resources are available to guide faculty in their teaching. One example, Gordon Uno's *Handbook on Teaching Undergraduate Science Courses: A Survival Training Manual,* discusses topics ranging from lecturing to organizing and assessing, and is especially helpful for new faculty (Uno, 1997). Several journals also publish information on science education. *The Journal of College Science Teaching* is published by the National Science Teachers Association and *The American Biology Teacher* is published by the National Association of Biology Teachers. More general information on teaching and education can be found in *The Chronicle of Higher Education* and the book *Tools for Teaching* by Barbara Gross Davis. Books are also available to assist faculty in changing their teaching approach. *Student-Active Science: Models of Innovation in College Science Teaching* (McNeal and D'Avanzo,

---

[3]Metacognition is the process of thinking about thoughts, for example being aware of how people think and learn. It can be thought of as a three-step process: developing a plan of action, monitoring the plan, and evaluating the plan. A concise explanation of one way to do this can be found at *http://www.ncrel.org/sdrs/areas/issues/students/learning/lr1metn.htm.*

1997) contains numerous examples of designing new courses, pathways to change, and methods for assessment. *Peer Instruction: A User's Manual* (Mazur, 1997) focuses on physics teaching, but contains descriptions of its primary approach for engaging students (the ConcepTest) and ideas for motivating students. *The Hidden Curriculum: Faculty-Made Tests in Science* (Tobias and Raphael, 1977) presents additional ideas for varying the lecture approach to teaching. The Proceedings of the 1999 Sigma Xi Forum present ideas for inquiry-based teaching, specifically addressing its use in large classrooms (Sigma Xi, 2000). Several Web sites list other resources that may be helpful: *www.academicinfo.net/biologyed.html* and *www.mcb. harvard.edu/BioLinks/EduRes.html*. There are also resources for faculty available on their own campuses, such as centers for teaching and learning or centers of teaching excellence.

Inquiry-Based Learning

An increasing number of today's college faculty recognize the significance of the research findings discussed in *How People Learn* and incorporate inquiry-based teaching and learning into their courses. The main idea of inquiry is for students to learn in the same way that scientists learn through research. Scientists ask questions, make observations, take measurements, analyze data, and repeat this process in an attempt to integrate new information. Students should be taught the way scientists think about the world, and how they analyze a scientific problem in particular. Inquiry advocates the use of this process for teaching in the classroom, lab, or field. Some essential features of classroom inquiry (use of evidence, framing of scientific questions, etc.) are listed in the NRC report *Inquiry and the National Science Education Standards* (NRC, 2000c). Although this report is written for elementary and high school science teachers, it contains good ideas for undergraduate faculty as well. The National Science Teachers Association has published a guide for faculty on how to use the ideas of the science education standards in the college classroom to increase student-centered and inquiry-based learning (Siebert and McIntosh, 2001). The NRC has plans to publish a volume focusing on inquiry in the undergraduate classroom through its Committee on Undergraduate Science Education Web site.

Inquiry-Based Learning via Undergraduate Research

Many of today's researchers were drawn to the excitement of biology by a mentor. Often that mentor was a faculty member who supervised an undergraduate laboratory project. For example, Mary Allen, the Jean Glasscock Professor of Biological Sciences and chair of the Department of Biological Sciences at Wellesley, said:

> I was an undergraduate studying chemistry at a large research university when I discovered, through a summer of mentored research, that I truly loved the excitement of discovering something new through research. I spent a summer driving around the state of Wisconsin in a University van, collecting large volumes of lake water, then taking them back to the lab and analyzing them and trying to get microbes to grow in them. It was a totally different, and a much more engaging experience, than sitting in lectures with 500 students and going to labs where I followed a cookbook method with some 24 other students. In doing research as an undergraduate, instead of only receiving information, I was engaged actively in the discovery and production of new knowledge, making an original intellectual or creative contribution to the discipline, and I loved it! (Distinguished Faculty Lecture, September 2000).

Participation in research by all students is a goal to which institutions should aspire. Research gives students a sense of empowerment over a body of knowledge and instills in them the confidence to succeed. This empowerment stems in large part from the intense professional relationship that develops between students and faculty mentors. Mentors and students share in the ownership of research in a manner that promotes mutual growth and learning in a relationship that grows and intensifies over time. It is evident from many quarters that such students develop a sustaining relationship with their faculty mentor, have strongly enriched and productive research experiences, and usually assume leadership roles in their research groups and departments as they progress toward graduation. Furthermore, the mentoring relationship that is established between a student and a faculty member is particularly effective at affirming the integration of that student into the culture of science. The highly significant benefits of undergraduate research are discussed further in Chapter 5.

While many institutions work hard to include all rising seniors in research programs, there is also a history of success with moving talented students into the laboratory at an early stage of their academic career. The committee believes that such relationships are important for all students and would be particularly meaningful for young women and students of color as they begin their journey into research and advanced science courses.

This is not a new idea, but is stressed in the belief that it has continuing relevance in today's colleges and universities. Numerous groups have already devoted considerable effort to promoting undergraduate research. The Council on Undergraduate Research (CUR) declares as its mission "to support and promote high-quality undergraduate student-faculty collaborative research and scholarship" (*http://www.cur.org/*). CUR focuses on primarily undergraduate institutions. A recent report by the Research Corporation examines the role of research in the physical sciences at undergraduate institutions; it documents model programs and discusses financial support for that research (Research Corporation and Doyle, 2000).

However, in spite of the overwhelming circumstantial evidence and broad-based agreement that undergraduate research is good pedagogy, the educational value of undergraduate research for students, and the impact of undergraduate research on faculty development as scholars and educators, has not been assessed in a systematic and intensive way. The Research Corporation report mentioned above, *Academic Excellence*, does examine such issues; in addition, another study in progress attempts to assess the value of undergraduate research (See Case Study #1).

Throughout this report, case studies are presented to elaborate on the ideas presented in the main text. The case studies are brief examples that provide more detail on a specific course, program, or approach as well as a source for further information. Information for the case studies came from committee members, panel members, and workshop speakers, as well as resources they cited and recommendations from HHMI and Project Kaleidoscope. In some cases, additional information was obtained from program directors or institutional Web sites.

Inquiry-Based Learning via Laboratory Courses

Many schools have trouble finding the resources to offer these types of experiences to all students. A host of infrastructure limitations, combined with an overwhelming number of biology students, restrict the number of students who can have opportunities for research experiences with independent work, at least early in their undergraduate careers. Institutions should be creative in finding ways to provide opportunities for research to all students. One way to share the excitement of biology with students is to replicate the idea of independent work within the context of courses by incorporating inquiry-based learning, project labs, and group assignments. The importance of a direct connection between teacher and student is not

CASE STUDY #1
Assessment of Undergraduate Research
Grinnell College, Harvey Mudd College, Hope College, Wellesley College

The results from this in-depth study will, hopefully, improve understanding of the impact that undergraduate research has on student learning and on development of faculty into teacher-scholars. Four liberal arts colleges have come together to assess their own undergraduate research programs in order to provide a database that will be useful not only for the further development of their own programs, but also to fuel an understanding of undergraduate research at other institutions. Grinnell College (IA), Harvey Mudd College (CA), Hope College (MI), and Wellesley College (MA) are all recognized by the NSF as leaders in undergraduate research. These institutions are among only 10 liberal arts institutions that received a 1999 NSF Award for the Integration of Research and Education. The assessment is being conducted using a grant provided by the NSF-ROLE (Research on Learning and Education) program. The study is both quantitative (through an in-depth questionnaire filled out by each student researcher) and qualitative (each student researcher at each institution will have undergone at least two or three confidential interviews during the assessment period). Student researchers are providing input on research activities from both the summer and the academic year, and on the impact of their research experiences on their individual career paths following graduation. Faculty members from these institutions are also participating. It is anticipated that the information gleaned from the faculty will provide a unique perspective on faculty career development as teacher-scholars and the effect that research collaborations with undergraduates have on that development.

The study is currently in Year 2 of a three-year effort, and the data for the initial two years of the assessment period are currently being analyzed in detail. The outcomes from this study will be disseminated in 2003. It is of importance not only because of the issues that it seeks to address in understanding the impact of undergraduate research, but also because it focuses directly upon the important issue of assessment of educational endeavors.

For more information: *https://www.fastlane.nsf.gov/servlet/ showaward? award=0087611* a new idea. It has been used in teaching for ages. However, it can be "discovered" as new by successive generations of teachers. In the preface of *The Feynman Lectures on Physics*, published in 1963, Richard Feynman discussed his experiences teaching introductory physics at the California Institute of Technology (Feynman et al., 1963). He taught 180 students in a large lecture hall. He struggled with how to reach students of varied backgrounds and abilities with the low level of feedback a faculty member receives from students in a large lecture. He concluded,

> there isn't any solution to this problem of education other than to realize that the best teaching can only be done when there is a direct individual relationship between a student and a good teacher—a situation in which the student discusses the ideas, thinks about things, and talks about the things. It's impossible to learn very much simply by sitting in a lecture, or even by simply doing the problems that are assigned. But in our modern times we have so many students to teach that we have to try to find some substitute for the ideal.

Drawing from Feynman's observations, this report attempts to provide guidance on more than just what "things" to think about and talk about, but also how to encourage students to do that thinking and talking and learning.

Studies and Reports on Inquiry-Based Learning

A study sponsored by the National Institute for Science Education in Madison, Wisconsin, found small group cooperative learning had a large positive effect on students' comprehension (O'Donnell et al., 1997). A 1995 convocation held by the NSF and the NRC, *From Analysis to Action* (NRC, 1996), stressed the need for inquiry-based approaches to the teaching of introductory science courses. In 1998, the Boyer Commission released a report, *Reinventing Undergraduate Education: A Blueprint for America's Research Universities* (Kenny and Boyer Commission on Educating Undergraduates in the Research University, 1998), which looked at all disciplines, not just the sciences. Their recommendations focused on making learning more research-focused, creating opportunities for interdisciplinary learning, and providing capstone experiences for seniors to help them integrate the knowledge they have gained throughout their college career. The NRC report *Transforming Undergraduate Education* suggests that these kinds of courses can also be very useful in the early years of college to help students see the relationships between different sets of knowledge so that they better understand why they need to take courses in subject areas that may at first seem indirectly related to their majors (NRC, 1999b).

In the early 1990s, a network of professional societies in biology set out to increase the attention paid to undergraduate education. Efforts by the Coalition for Education in the Life Sciences (CELS) led to the publication of a curricular framework for introductory biology. *Issues-Based Framework for Bio 101* (Coalition for Education in the Life Sciences, 1992) called for all students to receive an education in overarching issues in biology in the belief that this education is necessary to prepare them to participate fully in society. The group also published a monograph entitled *Professional Societies and the Faculty Scholar: Promoting Scholarship and Learning in the Life Sciences* (Coalition for Education in the Life Sciences, 1998). This monograph addresses issues of faculty development, including the way that "faculty find both cooperation and competition from many sources in their commitment to teaching." The cooperation or competition can come from within the department or professional society, from grant proposals to funding agencies, or from publications on education. The publication advocates that professional societies learn from each other and work together to promote the production and dissemination of educational materials and argues effectively that professional societies must play a leadership role in promoting faculty development. A 1999 report from the NRC, *Transforming Undergraduate Education in Science, Mathematics, Engineering, and Technology* (NRC, 1999b), addresses many of the larger institutional issues that must be solved to truly improve undergraduate science education. It calls for "post-secondary institutions to provide the rewards, recognition, resources, tools and infrastructure necessary to promote innovative and effective undergraduate science, mathematics, engineering and technology (SMET) teaching and learning" and provides strategies for achieving that goal.

This report builds on many aspects of these earlier works to offer an analysis of appropriate topics in each scientific discipline that have relevance to biology students. It proposes a variety of ways to improve interdisciplinary scientific education for future biomedical researchers. It provides guidance for faculty on ways to incorporate chemistry, physics, mathematics, computer science, and engineering into the undergraduate education of future biomedical researchers. Assessment measures must be an integral component of all attempts at curriculum reform, and, importantly, for the educational reforms identified and recommended in this report.

Recent changes in the practice of biological research and knowledge gained from education research are not adequately reflected in today's undergraduate biology classroom. Significant changes are necessary to prepare students to become biomedical researchers of the future. This report lays out a plan to transform undergraduate education in biology. Implementation of this plan will require more than tinkering around at the edges of the current system. It will require a dramatic change in the priority given to professional development for faculty. For it to succeed, faculty must engage themselves in a learning process to gain the skills and knowledge that will help their students learn. More importantly, college and university administrators must actively support faculty in these endeavors. Administrators must help faculty obtain the time and money to prepare and implement new ways of teaching science. However, even large increases in the time and money devoted to educational reform will not have an optimal impact if the academic culture does not begin to give a higher priority to education. Evidence given throughout this report supports the idea that interdisciplinary education is in the best interests of both undergraduates and their professors, and that science faculty should take responsibility for ensuring that their teaching is of the highest quality possible.

The committee also hopes that this report will stimulate institutions to carry out a comprehensive review of the educational experiences of undergraduate life science majors. These experiences include learning inside and outside of the classroom, the content covered, and the way in which it is taught. The report calls for colleges and universities to be more attentive to how their policies create incentives for faculty behavior that may encourage or discourage attention to teaching. Increasing the incentives for faculty to devote attention to teaching is necessary to facilitate ongoing efforts to provide a quality education for undergraduates. However, increased attention to teaching alone will not be enough; faculty must also have access to teaching resources and experts with knowledge of appropriate educational approaches.

STATISTICS ON BIOLOGY STUDENTS

This report focuses on preparing biomedical researchers, while recognizing that there are many other career options for biology students. NSF's *Science and Engineering Indicators* (National Science Foundation and National Science Board, 2000) predicts that the number of jobs for biological and medical scientists will grow from 110,000 in the year 2000 to 135,000 in the year 2010. In 1998 1.2 million bachelor's degrees were awarded in the United States, and 85,079 (7.1%) of those students majored in the life sciences (National Science Foundation and National Science Board, 2000). Comparison of the number of jobs and the number of majors reveals that most biology majors do not enter research as a career. However, surveys done in 1995-1996 showed that only 6% of life science graduates expected their bachelor's degree to be the end of their formal education. Thirty-eight percent planned to obtain masters, 29% doctorates, and 27% professional degrees. In the late 1990s, approximately 6,500 PhDs in the life sciences were granted each year. Among entering college students in the fall of 2001, 7% planned to major in a biological science (University of California et al., 2001). Only 2% of freshmen listed scientific researcher or college teacher as a probable career, 6% said physician, and almost 15% listed undecided.

Entering students encountered faculty who spent 57% of their time on teaching-related activities and 15% on research, although at research or doctoral institutions, and among full professors the amount of time devoted to teaching was lower (U.S. Department of Education, 2001). In the natural sciences approximately 86% of faculty reported lecturing as their primary method of instruction (U.S. Department of Education, 2001). Revised teaching approaches that appeal more to students may encourage more talented undergraduates to consider scientific careers.

ORIGIN OF BIO2010

In October 2000, the Board on Life Sciences of the National Research Council initiated this study, *Undergraduate Biology Education to Prepare Research Scientists for the 21st Century.* The idea for the study emerged from discussions between Dr. Bruce Alberts, President of the National Academy of Sciences, and officials at NIH and HHMI who were concerned about the undergraduate education of future researchers. Over the past decade, both organizations had observed increases in the amount of expertise in mathematics and the physical and information sciences required for biomedical research. NIH and HHMI committed to funding Bio2010, as this study came to be known, to examine ways of strengthening the chemistry, physics, engineering, mathematics, and computer science background of undergraduate biology majors in ways that would enable these students to make stronger interdisciplinary connections in their future research.

Bio2010 Objectives

The Committee on Undergraduate Biology Education to Prepare Research Scientists for the 21st Century (Bio2010) was charged with examining the formal undergraduate education, training, and experience required to prepare the next generation of life science majors with a particular emphasis on the preparation of students for careers in biomedical research. Another fundamental goal of the project was to identify the basic skills and concepts of mathematics, chemistry, physics, computer science, and engineering that will assist students in making novel interdisciplinary connections. The complete formal charge to the committee can be found in Appendix A. The Bio2010 committee was asked to produce an innovative and realizable action plan for modifying undergraduate biology education so that life science majors can begin their research careers better prepared for the challenges and opportunities of the next decade and beyond. Because the life sciences are so broadly defined, and because at the undergraduate level, it is difficult to separate those students who will become biomedical researchers from their classmates who will pursue a multitude of other career paths, the committee also considered the needs of students in other life science disciplines during their discussions. The Committee was asked, in considering the undergraduate biology education of future research scientists, to "emphasize preparing students for biomedical research" and to also evaluate "how preparation should be similar or different for other life science disciplines such as plant biology, population and evolutionary biology, and behavior and cognitive sciences." The Committee has deliberated on this question and has concluded that the best preparation for the biomedical research of the future is a broadly based education in biology with a strong foundation in the physical sciences and mathematics. A well-educated biology major should understand the principles of population and evolutionary biology, ecology, cognitive neurobiology, and plant biology, irrespective of his or her future research area. The connections between biomedical research and other sciences will become more intimate and mutually reinforcing in the years ahead. Most compelling, the fundamental unity of biology speaks strongly against the desirability of compartmentalization too early in one's education. The committee believes that the new biology curriculum proposed in this report will be of benefit to all future research biologists, not just those headed for biomedical research as it is known today.

The following questions guided the study:

- How will biology research be conducted in the future, and how should future approaches to research inform education in the life sciences?
- What fundamental skills and knowledge do undergraduates in the life sciences need to prepare them to become research scientists? How are those skills and knowledge best conveyed?
- What are the fundamental concepts of mathematics, chemistry, physics, computer science, and engineering that will assist students in making interdisciplinary connections?
- To what extent can these interdisciplinary skills and knowledge be taught in the context of central issues in biology? Should these skills and concepts be acquired through a restructuring of biology courses or through a broadening of the content and structure of courses in mathematics, chemistry, and physics?
- To the extent that portions of the desired curriculum are better treated in academic departments outside the life sciences, what are the best practices for collaborating with faculty in those departments to achieve mutually agreeable goals? What institutional barriers to collaboration exist and how have they been addressed in successful cases of curricular change? What incentives exist or might be created to overcome barriers to change?
- What innovative programs for teaching life science majors have been developed, and what can be learned from those programs?

Expertise of the Committee and Content Panels

An 11-member committee composed of leading scientists and educators in biology, the physical sciences, and mathematics undertook the study. All are practicing scientists with a strong interest and dedication to education. The committee did not include experts in learning theory and pedagogy as the charge stated that the study would focus on examples of concepts and courses that would promote interdisciplinary learning. This report is the result of a two-year process that they directed. Many of the ideas and recommendations presented here reinforce and build upon material from earlier reports by the NRC and others, particularly the ideas of mechanisms for improving undergraduate science education. In coming to the conclusions presented here, the committee began by discussing the overall state of biomedical research and undergraduate biology education. They canvassed their colleagues, educational experts, journal articles, and the Internet, gathering information on both traditional and innovative courses and curricula in undergraduate science. The committee used this informa-

03.96

tion to determine the most pressing issues for the report to address, and the types of scientists who should be invited to provide more specific input to the committee.

The committee also convened three advisory panels during the winter of 2001—in Chemistry, Physics and Engineering, and Mathematics and Computer Science—to provide expert advice on how to teach their respective disciplines to biology majors, both in biology classrooms and laboratories and in introductory courses of their respective disciplines. The panel participants were chosen from a large pool of names provided by NAS section liaisons, representatives of professional societies and educational associations, NRC staff, and others. The panel participants were also asked to recommend presenters for a workshop. The panels each consisted of seven to ten members drawn from diverse institutions of higher education and led by a Bio2010 committee member with expertise in the respective discipline (see Appendix C). They provided written accounts of their findings and recommendations to the Bio2010 Committee.

Workshop on Innovative Undergraduate Biology Education

Another important source of information and advice for the committee was the "Workshop on Innovative Undergraduate Biology Education," which was organized by the Bio2010 Committee and held in Snowmass, Colorado, in August 2001. Participants were selected as described above for the panels. Sixteen participants from colleges, universities, foundations, and the federal government were invited to share with the Bio2010 Committee their experiences and opinions on methods for teaching undergraduate science (See Appendix G). In designing the workshop, the committee first considered the working papers prepared by the panels. They discussed the issues that had arisen during the panel meetings, looking for both similarities and differences between disciplines. They selected issues for the workshop that they wanted to learn more about. They identified individuals to invite from the large pool of suggestions already collected and solicited additional names from experts in the relevant fields under consideration. The participants in the workshop were provided with the working papers of the panels and asked to provide comments on them to the committee. They also presented material on their own educational endeavors, suggested relevant case studies, and recommended other sources of information for the committee as it completed its report.

2

A New Biology Curriculum

RECOMMENDATION #1

Given the profound changes in the nature of biology and how biological research is performed and communicated, each institution of higher education should reexamine its current courses and teaching approaches (as described in this report) to see if they meet the needs of today's undergraduate biology students. Those selecting the new approaches should consider the importance of building a strong foundation in mathematics, physical, and information sciences to prepare students for research that is increasingly interdisciplinary in character. The implementation of new approaches should be accompanied by a parallel process of assessment, to verify that progress is being made toward the institutional goal of student learning.

This chapter presents ideas for ways to enhance undergraduate education in biology. However, the committee recognizes that the specific examples described here are only a subset of the many possible ways to increase interdisciplinary learning. The list of concepts that follow are lengthy. There is no way to incorporate all of this material into one or even several courses. The lists are presented as concepts that would be helpful to future biomedical researchers, if they were introduced at some point during a four-year undergraduate program. Many but not all would be helpful to other biology students who are focusing their studies on areas of life sciences such as population biology, plant biology, or cognitive science. These non-biomedical biologists would benefit from the increased attention to biological concepts in their other science courses. All biology students should study some of the concepts in depth as undergraduates. The specific concepts studied in detail by any individual student will depend on their interests, career goals, and the course offerings and course content available at their own school. Beyond the specific content of what they learn, students need hands-on experience with experimental inquiry and research starting early in their undergraduate careers. Their undergraduate experience should give them a sense of the power and beauty of science that takes full advantage of the richness of ideas and tools provided by a broad range of disciplines.

The concepts are presented at the beginning of this chapter and potential curricula at the end. The concepts are presented first so that faculty can consider how they might be incorporated into the courses offered. An evolutionary biologist teaching introductory biology will select different concepts from these lists than a developmental biologist teaching the same course. Either set of choices can improve interdisciplinary training of students and contribute to the creation of graduates who think more broadly. Ideally the changes will also help students see the connections between their different science courses and relate the topics to their own lives. Most biology students will not take such intensive schedules as presented in the sample curricula, and it is certainly possible to become a biomedical researcher without all of this background. However, the committee feels that future biomedical researchers, and possibly many other types of researchers, would be better prepared to contribute to interdisciplinary breakthroughs with such a background.

Because of the striking advances in contemporary biology, those who plan to carry out biological research will need to access a broader range of concepts and skills than did past generations. The modern biologist uses a wide array of advanced techniques, ranging from special measuring instruments, novel imaging systems, computer methods, and quantitative analytical tools and models. Understanding and effectively applying these techniques requires knowledge from outside of the biological sciences. Furthermore, the analysis of biological systems, with their web of complex interactions, will require the design of new theoretical approaches. To meet the challenges of the new biology, the committee believes that all future biological researchers will need concepts and skills drawn from a range of scientific disciplines that must be broader than what has been expected up to now. Because of biology's great diversity, specific requirements will differ among the various subareas of biological research, and no one individual is expected to be equally competent in all the relevant areas of physics, chemistry, mathematics, and engineering. Nevertheless, as a guide to the key biologically relevant ideas in these areas, and to stimulate discussion of what constitutes the core knowledge for the new biological curricula, the report begins by offering what is believed to be the central concepts of chemistry, physics, engineering, and mathematics that are most relevant to biology. Following these concepts are four examples of potential undergraduate biology curricula that would be appropriate for future biomedical researchers. These examples are not meant to discourage the use of alternate curricula that also cover the content of mathematics and physical and information sciences. Many of the courses listed have familiar titles in order to illustrate that many of the recommendations found in this report could be implemented through existing courses. However, the content of the courses would likely be altered to increase the integration of the different sciences.

Throughout this report the committee uses the term "quantitative biology" to refer to a biology in which mathematics and computing serve as essential tools in framing experimental questions, analyzing experimental data, generating models, and making predictions that can be tested. In quantitative biology, the multifaceted relationships between molecules, cells, organisms, species, and communities are characterized and comprehended by finding structure in massive data sets that span different levels of biological organization. It is a science in which new computational, physical, and chemical tools are sought and applied to gain a deeper and more coherent understanding of the biological world that has strong predictive power.

Communicating how scientific advances and discoveries are made is a crucial part of undergraduate scientific education. First, exposure to the experimental and conceptual basis of key discoveries gives students a deeper understanding of scientific principles. Reading a classic paper can give students a sense of scientific inquiry at its best. Students can gain much by considering questions such as: What motivated the study? How were the experiments designed? What new experimental methods or analytical approaches were needed? How surprising was the outcome? How did the discovery influence the future course of science? Second, by exploring how discoveries are made, students acquire an appreciation of the history and culture of science. Science becomes a human endeavor that spans time and space. Third, scientific discoveries are inspirational. They stimulate students, demonstrate the importance of the prepared mind, and convey a sense of adventure and excitement.

Scientific discoveries and how they were made can be communicated in many mutually reinforcing ways. First, lectures can be made more vivid and engaging by presenting carefully chosen exemplars of the process of discovery, such as Darwin's finches, Mendel's peas, Morgan's flies, and McClintock's maize. Roentgen's discovery of x-rays, von Laue's and the Braggs' use of them to reveal atomic structure, and Watson and Crick's reading of x-ray diffraction patterns in discovering the DNA double helix could be presented as a remarkable sequence of major scientific advances over more than a half century that led to the birth of a new biology. Second, many textbooks contain lucid accounts of the process of discovery that are interwoven with expositions of basic principles. Students should also be encouraged to read the full text of classic papers, which can be made accessible by posting them on the Web. Third, problem sets included in texts or written by instructors for their courses can be choice devices for exploring scientific advances that are inherently quantitative, such as the Hardy-Weinberg equilibrium and Shannon's measure of information. Fourth, laboratory courses can motivate an experiment by recounting the historical background. For example, a biochemistry laboratory experiment on a glycolytic enzyme could begin with the Buchners' discovery of fermentation in a cell-free yeast extract, a chemistry laboratory experiment on halogenation with Scheele's discovery of chlorine, and a physics laboratory experiment on lasers with Einstein's prediction of stimulated emission. Indeed, a classic discovery can be the basis of an extended experiment in which students explore new terrain, as in the use of the Hill reaction (light-induced electron transfer in illuminated chloroplasts), to find herbicides (an experiment in the interdisciplinary laboratory course described in Case Study #6).

Noteworthy current advances should be presented along with classic discoveries. The covers of major journals often have striking images depicting important research findings. They can be used as evocative starting points in lectures and group discussions to motivate as well as inform students. For example, the recent discovery of fossils suggesting that the divergence between the human and chimpanzee lineages occurred earlier than previously thought (Brunet et al., 2002) would inform and enliven the teaching of human origins, especially if the paper were contrasted with previous estimates of the time of divergence based on molecular clocks.

Future research biologists should also be exposed to scientific controversies and their resolution.

CONCEPTS AND SKILLS FOR THE NEW CURRICULUM

The concepts presented in this chapter are the end result of the long study process described in Chapter 1. Initially the committee examined the requirements for biology majors at 12 institutions of various types around the country. They compared this information to the requirements for biology majors at their own college or university and discussed some of the similarities and differences. The committee also discussed the desired characteristics for the invited experts who would participate in the panels on Chemistry, Physics and Engineering, and Mathematics and Computer Science. They selected faculty members who covered the subdisciplines within each panel's charge, and those who are known for their teaching. The following lists of concepts owe much to the ideas shared by the panel members during their respective meetings. Each panel approached its task from a different perspective, and hence created slightly different types of recommendations. The panel members considered the way their discipline is currently taught to biology students, at their own institution and others with which they are familiar. In assembling their recommendations, they considered the course requirements, the content of those courses, the content that is most relevant to biology students, and to some degree the way in which the material is taught (lectures, seminars, laboratories). The committee as a whole went through a similar process to create the list of biology concepts presented below. In preparing the final concept lists for the report, the committee has attempted to structure the lists in a way that stresses their pertinence to interdisciplinary research and education.

In addition to the concepts presented on the following lists, the committee recognizes that future biologists, and indeed all future workers and citizens, will also need more general skills. Science faculty are not required to leave the teaching of reading, writing, critical thinking, and communication skills solely to the humanities and social sciences faculty. For example, incorporating the writing of grant proposals, or the scientific component of a business proposal for a biotech start-up, into a course provides useful experience requiring knowledge of both scientific ideas and other skills. These types of activities also provide an opportunity for students to consider the interplay between scientific discovery and society, including the importance of the scientific method and scientific ethics.

Biology

RECOMMENDATION #1.1

Understanding the unity and diversity of life requires mastery of a set of fundamental concepts. This understanding will be greatly enhanced if biology courses build on material begun in other science courses to expose students to the ideas of modeling and analyzing biological and other systems.

Biological systems show remarkable unity at the molecular and cellular levels, reflecting their common ancestry. Variations on this unity lead to the extraordinary diversity of individual organisms. In order for biology students to understand the unifying features of the biological concepts listed below, the concepts must be taught in multiple contexts. Biology faculty should consider the various points in their courses at which the concepts will fit. They should also consider the concept lists for chemistry, physics, and mathematics that follow and the ways in which those ideas could be incorporated into biology courses. In order for biology students to receive a truly interdisciplinary education, cooperation between departments will be necessary. It is the responsibility of the biology faculty to make active outreach efforts to colleagues in other departments by offering to work together on mechanisms for incorporating biological concepts and examples into non-biology courses.

Concepts of Biology

Central Themes

• All living things have evolved from a common ancestor, through processes that include natural selection and genetic drift acting on heritable genetic variation.

• Biological systems obey the laws of chemistry and physics.

• Structural complexity and information content are built up by combining simpler subunits into multiple complex combinations.

• Understanding biological systems requires both reductionist and holistic thinking because novel properties emerge as simpler units assemble into more complex structures.

• Living systems are far from equilibrium. They utilize energy, largely derived from photosynthesis, which is stored in high-energy bonds or ionic concentration gradients. The release of this energy is coupled to thermodynamically unfavorable reactions to drive biological processes.

• Although fundamental molecular and cellular processes are conserved, biological systems and organisms are extraordinarily diverse. Unlike atoms and simple molecules studied in chemistry and physics, no two cells are identical.

• Biological systems maintain homeostasis by the action of complex regulatory systems. These are often networks of interconnecting partially redundant systems to make them stable to internal or external changes.

• Cells are fundamental units of living systems. Three fundamental cell types have evolved: bacteria, archea, and eukaryotes.

• Living organisms have behavior, which can be altered by experience in many species.

• Information encoded in DNA is organized into genes. These heritable units use RNA as informational intermediates to encode protein sequences, which become functional on folding into distinctive three-dimensional structures. In some situations RNA itself has catalytic activity.

• Most biological processes are controlled by multiple proteins, which assemble into modular units to carry out and coordinate complex functions.

• Lipids assemble with proteins to form membranes, which surround cells to separate them from their environment. Membranes also form distinct compartments within eukaryotic cells.

• Communication networks within and between cells, and between organisms, enable multicellular organisms to coordinate development and function.

• In multicellular organisms, cells divide and differentiate to form tissues, organs, and organ systems with distinct functions. These differences arise primarily from changes in gene expression.

• Many diseases arise from disruption of cellular communication and coordination by infection, mutation, chemical insult, or trauma.

• Groups of organisms exist as species, which include interbreeding populations sharing a gene pool.

• Populations of species interact with one another and the environment to form interdependent ecosystems with flow of energy and materials between multiple levels.

• Humans, as well as many other species, are members of multiple ecosystems. They have the capacity to disrupt or preserve the ecosystems upon which they depend.

Chemistry

RECOMMENDATION #1.2

*The committee recommends that biology majors receive a thorough educa-
tion in chemistry, including general chemistry and aspects of organic chemistry,
physical chemistry, analytical chemistry, and biochemistry, incorporated into a
new course or courses. They should master the chemistry concepts listed below.
Biology faculty should work in concert with their chemistry colleagues to help
design chemistry curricula that will not only foster growth of aspiring chemists,
but also stimulate biology majors as well as students majoring in other disciplines. Furthermore, chemistry faculty must work with biologists to find ways to
collaborate on the incorporation of chemistry concepts, and those of other scientific disciplines, into their teaching of biology. Learning biology should not be
dependent upon chemistry but, rather, integrated with it. Biology students
should begin their study of chemistry in the first year so that they will acquire a
strong foundation in chemistry before starting their study of chemically based
aspects of biology.*

Chemistry has always been an important sister science to biology, especially to biochemistry and medicine. Today, modern molecular biology and
cell biology focus on understanding the chemistry of genes and of cell structure. In the applied area, for example, chemistry is central to modern
agriculture. Biomedical engineering draws on chemistry for new materials.
It is evident that future research biologists will need to have a thorough
grounding in chemistry to make their research possible and to understand
the work of others. Such a grounding in general chemistry and organic
chemistry has historically required at least three semesters of chemistry
courses, but could require fewer following an integrated restructuring.
There are many combinations of courses that would allow students to learn
these chemical concepts. In the traditional program, a full year of general
chemistry is followed by a full year of organic chemistry, and then by physical chemistry.

Regardless of when it is taught, organic chemistry should include material on the principal biomolecules, including heterocyclic chemistry and
the chemistry of phosphate esters. The role of these biomolecules in biology is so important that they should not be omitted, as too frequently
occurs. Furthermore, including a description of the biochemical versions of
displacement reactions, aldol and Claisen condensations, and free radical
reactions will add interest for all students, not just biologists.

Concepts of Chemistry

Atoms
- Periodic table, trends (size, electronic properties, isoelectronic systems)
- Orbitals and electronic configuration
- Nuclear chemistry

Molecules
- Lewis structures
- Molecular properties (shape, dipole moments, bond energies)
- Bonding models (valence bond theory, molecular orbital theory)
- Molecular interactions (ion pair, hydrogen bond, van der Waals)
- Metal ions and metal complexes
- Resonance and electron delocalization
- Computational methods and modeling

Water and Aqueous Solutions
- Structure and polarity of liquid water
- Ionic compounds in aqueous solutions
- Acid-base equilibria, pH, pK, indicators
- Hydrophobic effect

Chemical Reactions
- Stoichiometry
- Hydrocarbons, heterocycles, and functional groups
- Reaction types (acid-base, redox, addition, elimination, substitution)
- Reactive intermediates: carbocations, carbanions, enols, enolates, free radicals
- Mechanisms of selected classes of chemical reactions

Energetics and Equilibria
- Enthalpy, entropy, and free energy
- Equilibrium constant
- Temperature dependence of equilibria
- Electrochemistry, electrochemical cells, Nernst equation
- Boltzmann distribution

Reaction Kinetics
- Reaction rate laws and kinetic order
- Transition states
- Temperature dependence of kinetics
- Catalysis, enzyme-catalyzed reactions, and the Michaelis-Menten equation
- Diffusion-limited reactions
- Thermodynamic versus kinetic stability

Biomolecules
- Building blocks: amino acids, nucleotides, carbohydrates, fatty acids
- Biopolymers: proteins, nucleic acids, polysaccharides
- Three-dimensional structure of biological macromolecules
- Molecular assemblies: micelles, monolayers, biological membranes
- Solid-phase synthesis of oligonucleotides and peptides
- Combinatorial synthesis
- Spectroscopic reporters

Analyzing Molecules and Reactions
- Mass spectrometry
- Absorption and emission spectroscopy (UV, visible, infrared)
- NMR spectroscopy
- Diffraction (x-ray, neutron, electron)
- Electron microscopy and scanning probe microscopy
- Separation methods: chromatography, electrophoresis, and centrifugation
- Isotopic tracers and radioactivity

Materials
- Metals
- Properties and synthesis of polymers
- Conductors, insulators, and semiconductors

A list of questions useful in teaching these concepts is presented in Appendix D.

Physics

RECOMMENDATION #1.3

The principles of physics are central to the understanding of biological processes, and are increasingly important in sophisticated measurements in biology. The committee recommends that life science majors master the key physics concepts listed below. Experience with these principles provides a simple context in which to learn the relationship between observations and mathematical description and modeling.

The typical calculus-based introductory physics course taught today was designed to serve the needs of physics, mathematics, and engineering students. It allocates a major block of time to electromagnetic theory and to many details of classical mechanics. In so doing, it does not provide the time needed for in-depth descriptions of the equally basic physics on which students can build an understanding of biology. By emphasizing exactly solvable problems, the course rarely illustrates the ways that physics can be applied to more recalcitrant problems. Illustrations involving modern biology are rarely given, and computer simulations are usually absent. Collective behaviors and systems far from equilibrium are not a traditional part of introductory physics. However, the whole notion of emergent behavior, pattern formation, and dynamical networks is so central to understanding biology, where it occurs in an extremely complex context, that it should be introduced first in physical systems, where all interactions and parameters can be clearly specified, and quantitative study is possible.

Concepts of Physics

Motion, Dynamics, and Force Laws
- Measurement: physical quantities, units, time/length/mass, precision
- Equations of motion: position, velocity, acceleration, motion under gravity
- Newton's laws: force, mass, acceleration, springs and related material: stiffness, damping, exponential decay, harmonic motion
- Gravitational and spring potential energy, kinetic energy, power, heat from dissipation, work
- Electrostatic forces, charge, conductors/insulators, Coulomb's law
- Electric potential, current, units, Ohm's law

- Capacitors, R and RC circuits
- Magnetic forces and magnetic fields
- Magnetic induction and induced currents

Conservation Laws and Gobal Constraints
- Conservation of energy and momentum
- Conservation of charge
- First and Second Laws of thermodynamics

Thermal Processes at the Molecular Level
- Thermal motions: Brownian motion, thermal force (collisions), temperature, equilibrium
- Boltzmann's law, kT, examples
- Ideal gas statistical concepts using Boltzmann's law, pressure
- Diffusion limited dynamics, population dynamics

Waves, Light, Optics, and Imaging
- Oscillators and waves
- Geometrical optics: rays, lenses, mirrors
- Optical instruments: microscopes and microscopy
- Physical optics: interference and diffraction
- X-ray scattering and structure determination
- Particle in a box; energy levels; spectroscopy from a quantum viewpoint
- Other microscopies: electron, scanning tunneling, atomic force

Collective Behaviors and Systems far from Equilibrium
- Liquids, laminar flow, viscosity, turbulence
- Phase transitions, pattern formation, and symmetry breaking
- Dynamical networks: electrical, neural, chemical, genetic

Engineering

RECOMMENDATION #1.4

The committee recommends that life science majors be exposed to engineering principles and analysis. This does not necessarily require that they take a course in a school of engineering; courses in physics, biology, and other departments can provide exposure to these concepts. Students should have the opportunity to participate in laboratories that give them hands-on experience, so that they may learn about the functioning of complex systems, especially as they relate to the basic principles of physical science, mathematics, and modeling. Basic courses in physics and engineering should be developed specifically for life sciences students; these courses could be taught in either the physics or the biology department. This could be complemented exceptionally well by biology lecture or laboratory courses that assist students in their understanding of principles of physics and engineering (e.g., a unit on biomechanics taught in a physiology or anatomy course).

Biology increasingly involves the analysis of complex systems. Understanding function at the systems level requires a way of thinking that is common to engineers. Creating (or re-creating) function by building a complex system and getting it to work provides compelling proof that the scientist understands the essential building blocks and how they work in synchrony. Organisms can be analyzed in terms of subsystems having particular functions. To understand system function in biology in a predictive and quantitative fashion, it is necessary to describe and model how the system function results from the properties of its constituent elements. One approach to the study of biology is as a problem in reverse engineering. Manufactured systems are easier to understand than biological systems, because they have no unknown components, and their design principles can be explicitly stated. It is easiest to learn how to analyze systems through investigating how manufactured systems achieve their designed purpose, how their function depends on properties of their components, and how function can be reliable even with imperfect components. As an example, a quantitative understanding of a cell-signaling chemical network involves the concepts of negative feedback, gain, signal-to-noise, bandwidth, and cross-talk. These concepts are simple to experience in the context of how an electrical amplifier can be built from components. Similarly, an effort to understand the locomotion of insects might be preceded by a laboratory involving an analysis of a simple legged robot. In such a system, the description of the muscles (activators) and control signals is completely known, and the relation between the laws of physics and the problem of controlling directed movements can be seen clearly.

Examples of Engineering Topics Suitable for Inclusion in a Biology Curriculum

- The blood circulatory system and its control; fluid dynamics; pressure and force balance.

- Swimming, flying, walking, dynamical description, energy requirements, actuators, control. Material properties of biological systems and how their structure relates to their function (e.g., wood, hair, cell membranes, cartilage).
- Long range neuron signals; physical necessity of repeaters (e.g., nodes of Ranvier), engineering advantage of pulse coding, action potential generation, information transmission and errors.
- Shapes of cells: force balance, hydrostatic pressure, elasticity of membrane and effects of the spatial dependence of elasticity; cytoskeletal force effects on shape.

One such effort illustrates the interactions of the engineering and science involved, and makes it clear that the subject can be examined in enough detail to teach essential ideas honestly. A "long range neural signals" section might begin with the electrical conductivity of salt water, of the lipid cell membrane, and the electrical capacitance of the cell membrane. It would next develop the simple equations for the attenuation of a voltage applied across the membrane at one end of an axon "cylinder" with distance down the axon, and the effect of membrane capacitance on signal dynamics for time-varying signals. After substituting numbers, it becomes clear that amplifiers will be essential. Real systems are always noisy and imperfect; amplifiers have limited dynamical range; and the combination of these facts makes sending of an analog voltage signal through a large number of amplifiers essentially impossible. Pulse coding information escapes that problem (all long distance communication is digital these days). How are "pulses" generated by a cell? This would lead to the power supply needed by an amplifier—ion pumps, and the Nernst potential. How are action potentials generated? A first example of the transduction of an analog quantity into pulses might be stick-slip fraction, in which a block resting on a table and pulled by a weak spring whose end is steadily moved, moves in "jumps" whose distance is always the same. This introduction to nonlinear dynamics contains the essence of how an action potential is generated. The "negative resistance" of the sodium channels in a neuron membrane provides the same kind of "breakdown" phenomenon. Stability and instabilities (static and dynamic) of nonlinear dynamical systems can be analyzed, and finally the Hodgkin Huxley equations illustrated. The material is an excellent source of imaginative laboratories involving electrical measurements, circuits, dynamical systems, batteries and the Nernst potential, and information and noise, and classical mechanics. It has great potential for simulations of systems a little too complicated for complete mathematical analysis, and thus is ideal for teaching simulation as a tool for understanding.

Many topics in biology interact with the engineering viewpoint in such a fashion.

Mathematics and Computer Science

RECOMMENDATION #1.5

Quantitative analysis, modeling, and prediction play increasingly significant day-to-day roles in today's biomedical research. To prepare for this sea change in activities, biology majors headed for research careers need to be educated in a more quantitative manner, and such quantitative education may require the development of new types of courses. The committee recommends that all biology majors master the concepts listed below. In addition, the committee recommends that life science majors become sufficiently familiar with the elements of programming to carry out simulations of physiological, ecological, and evolutionary processes. They should be adept at using computers to acquire and process data, carry out statistical characterization of the data and perform statistical tests, and graphically display data in a variety of representations. Furthermore, students should also become skilled at using the Internet to carry out literature searches, locate published articles, and access major databases.

The elucidation of the sequence of the human genome has opened new vistas and has highlighted the increasing importance of mathematics and computer science in biology. The intense interest in genetic, metabolic, and neural networks reflects the need of biologists to view and understand the coordinated activities of large numbers of components of the complex systems underlying life. Biology students should be prepared to carry out *in silico* (computer) experiments to complement *in vitro* and *in vivo* experiments. It is essential that biology undergraduates become quantitatively literate. The concepts of rate of change, modeling, equilibria and stability, structure of a system, interactions among components, data and measurement, visualizing, and algorithms are among those most important to the curriculum. Every student should acquire the ability to analyze issues arising in these contexts in some depth, using analytical methods (e.g., pencil and paper), appropriate computational tools, or both. The course of study would include aspects of probability, statistics, discrete models, linear algebra, calculus and differential equations, modeling, and programming.

Concepts of Mathematics and Computer Science

Calculus
- Complex numbers
- Functions
- Limits
- Continuity
- The integral
- The derivative and linearization
- Elementary functions
- Fourier series
- Multidimensional calculus: linear approximations, integration over multiple variables

Linear Algebra
- Scalars, vectors, matrices
- Linear transformations
- Eeigenvalues and eigenvectors
- Invariant subspaces

Dynamical Systems
- Continuous time dynamics—equations of motion and their trajectories
- Test points, limit cycles, and stability around them
- Phase plane analysis
- Cooperativity, positive feedback, and negative feedback
- Multistability
- Discrete time dynamics — mappings, stable points, and stable cycles
- Sensitivity to initial conditions and chaos

Probability and Statistics
- Probability distributions
- Random numbers and stochastic processes
- Covariation, correlation, and independence
- Error likelihood

Information and Computation
- Algorithms (with examples)
- Computability

- Optimization in mathematics and computation
- "Bits": information and mutual information

Data Structures
- Metrics: generalized 'distance' and sequence comparisons
- Clustering
- Tree-relationships
- Graphics: visualizing and displaying data and models for conceptual understanding

Additional Quantitative Principles Useful to Biology Students

Rate of Change
- This can be a specific (e.g., per capita) rate of change or a total rate of change of some system component.
- Discrete rates of change arise in difference equations, which have associated with them an inherent time-scale.
- Continuous rates of change arise as derivatives or partial derivatives, representing instantaneous (relative to the units in which time is scaled) rates.

Modeling
- The process of abstracting certain aspects of reality to include in the simplifications of reality we call models.
- Scale (spatial and temporal)—different questions arise on different scales.
- What is included (system variables) depends on the questions addressed, as does the hierarchical level in which the problem is framed (e.g., molecular, cellular, organismal).
- There are trade-offs in modeling—no one model can address all questions. These trade-offs are between generality, precision, and realism.
- Evaluating models depends in part on the purpose for which the model was constructed. Models oriented toward prediction of specific phenomena may require formal statistical validation methods, while models that wish to elucidate general patterns of system response may require corroboration with the available observed patterns.

Equilibria and Stability
- Equilibria arise when a process (or several processes) rate of change is zero.
- There can be more than one equilibrium. Multiple stable states (e.g., long-term patterns that are returned to following a perturbation of the system) are typical of biological systems. The system dynamics may drive the process to any of these depending on initial conditions and history (e.g., the order of any sequence of changes in the system may affect the outcomes).
- Equilibria can be dynamic, so that a periodic pattern of system response may arise. This period pattern may be stable in that for some range of initial conditions, the system approaches this period pattern.
- There are numerous notions of stability, including not just whether a system that is perturbed from an equilibrium returns to it, but also how the system returns (e.g., how rapidly it does so).
- Modifying some system components can lead to destabilization of a previously stable equilibrium, possibly generating entirely new equilibria with differing stability characteristics. These bifurcations of equilibria arise in many nonlinear systems typical in biology.

Structure
- Grouping components of a system affects the kinds of questions addressed and the data required to parameterize the system.
- Choosing different aggregated formulations (by sex, age, size, physiological state, activity state) can expand or limit the questions that can be addressed, and data availability can limit the ability to investigate effects of structure.
- Geometry of the aggregation can affect the resulting formulation.
- Symmetry can be useful in many biological contexts to reduce the complexity of the problem, and situations in which symmetry is lost (symmetry-breaking) can aid in understanding system response.

Interactions
- There are relatively few ways for system components to interact. Negative feedbacks arise through competitive and predator-prey type interactions, positive feedback through mutualistic or commensal ones.
- Some general properties can be derived based upon these (e.g., two-

species competitive interactions), but even relatively few interacting system components can lead to complex dynamics.
- Though ultimately everything is hitched to everything else, significant effects are not automatically transferred through a connected system of interacting components—locality can matter.
- Sequences of interactions can determine outcomes—program order matters.

Data and Measurement
- Only a few basic data types arise (numeric, ordinal, categorical), but these will often be interconnected and expanded (e.g., as vectors or arrays).
- Consistency of the units with which one measures a system is important.
- A variety of statistical methods exist to characterize single data sets and to make comparisons between data sets. Using such methods with discernment takes practice.

Stochasticity
- In a stochastic process, individual outcomes cannot be predicted with certainty. Rather, these outcomes are determined randomly according to a probability distribution that arises from the underlying mechanisms of the process. Probabilities for measurements that are continuous (height, weight, etc.), and those that are discrete (sex, cell type) arise in many biological contexts.
- Risk can be identified and estimated.
- There are ways to determine if an experimental result is significant.
- There are instances when stochasticity is significant and averages are not sufficient.

Visualizing
- There are diverse methods to display data.
- Simple line and bar graphs are often not sufficient.
- Nonlinear transformations can yield new insights.

Algorithms
- These are rules that determine the types of interactions in a system, how decisions are made, and the time course of system response.
- These can be thought of as a sequence of actions similar to a com-

puter program, with all the associated options such as assignments, if-then loops, and while-loops.

Using Computers

Many of the concepts above deal with types of analysis and modeling that require knowledge of computer programming. However, there is another aspect of computing that is important for the future research biologist: the use of computers as tools. Computer use is a fact of life for all modern life scientists. Exposure during the early years of their undergraduate careers will help life science students use current computer methods and learn how to exploit emerging computer technologies as they arise. As computer power continues to grow rapidly, applications that were available only on supercomputers a few years ago can now be used on relatively inexpensive personal computers. Computers are essential today for obtaining information from databases (e.g., genetic data from Genbank), establishing relationships (e.g., using the BLAST algorithm to quantitate the similarity of a given DNA or protein sequence to all known sequences), deducing patterns (e.g., clustering genes that are regulated in concert), carrying out statistical tests, preparing plots and other graphics for presentation, and writing manuscripts for publication. Furthermore, computers are playing a central role in the laboratory in controlling equipment, obtaining data from measuring devices, and carrying out real-time analysis (e.g., image acquisition in confocal fluorescence microscopy). Research biologists are increasingly acquiring and analyzing vast amounts of data (e.g., the degree of expression of tens of thousands of genes in multiple cellular states). They will need to be conversant with new theoretical and modeling approaches to come to grips with the interplay of many simultaneously interacting components of complex systems.

Many analyses of biological data can be accomplished with existing programs (e.g., BLAST). However, being able to modify or construct applications is necessary in many research areas. Learning how a computer application is developed provides students with insight into the software they use. Computer understanding can be taught by providing experiences in computer programming, teaching about computer algorithms, and how to construct simple simulations. This familiarity could be accomplished by exposing students to programming in higher-level languages such as Matlab, Perl, or C.

The Internet is increasingly becoming the primary source of information for life scientists. Databases in a variety of areas (e.g., genomics, global warming, population dynamics) provide integrative frameworks that are valuable for addressing important biological issues. Becoming fully conversant with databases such as the National Center for Biotechnology Information (NCBI) is important for all biology majors. NCBI's mission is to develop new information technologies to aid in the understanding of fundamental molecular and genetic processes that control health and disease.

Searchable databases at NCBI's Web site (*http://www.ncbi.nlm.nih.gov*) include Genbank (all publicly available DNA sequences), PubMed (access to more than 11 million Medline citations of biomedical literature, including links to full text articles), BLAST (Basic Local Alignment Search Tool for carrying out similarity searches of DNA or protein query sequences), Taxonomy (a wide range of taxonomic information at the molecular level), and Structure (database of three-dimensional structure of biological macromolecules and tools for visualization and comparative analysis). Major model organism databases such as Fly Base (*www.flybase.org*) are useful, and The Interactive Fly (*http://sdb.bio.purdue.edu/fly/aimain/laahome.htm*) is a related learning tool.

Sites such as PubMed are essential for searching the literature and valuable for linking to full-text publications. Students should learn how to obtain different kinds of information from Web sites (e.g., DNA and protein sequences, atomic coordinates, phylogenetic relationships, functional anatomy, and biogeographic ecosystem data) and how to make information available to others over the Web (e.g., depositing new DNA sequences in Genbank). In addition, students should learn about mechanisms (e.g., peer review) of evaluating and increasing the reliability of information obtained on the Web.

Students should have experience operating lab equipment controlled by computer, and observe or attempt modification of the settings or the programming to fit the needs of the experiment. This type of experience is important for demonstrating that biological research is not constrained to the use of preexisting applications and materials. New approaches and equipment are developed regularly.

DESIGNING NEW CURRICULA SUITABLE FOR VARIOUS TYPES OF INSTITUTIONS

RECOMMENDATION #2

Concepts, examples, and techniques from mathematics, and the physical and information sciences should be included in biology courses, and biological concepts and examples should be included in other science courses. Faculty in biology, mathematics, and physical sciences must work collaboratively to find ways of integrating mathematics and physical sciences into life science courses as well as providing avenues for incorporating life science examples that reflect the emerging nature of the discipline into courses taught in mathematics and physical sciences.

Suggestions are provided here for integrating physical science and mathematics more fully into a biology education. Each institution will need to evaluate these recommendations in light of its own particular circumstances. Decisions will be influenced by many factors, including the size and expertise of the faculty, number of life science majors, and number of students from other science majors enrolled in biology courses. Consideration will also need to be given to the available resources, cooperation from other departments and the administration, and the need for curricular change to keep up with the dynamic growth of the discipline of biology. Regardless of individual circumstances, all institutions are capable of beginning the process of change by adding interdisciplinary examples to existing courses in relevant disciplines to emphasize the integrative nature of the biological sciences with mathematics and physical science. Chapter 3 presents case studies and ideas for courses that promote interdisciplinary learning.

The courses required of a biology major today typically consist of one year of physics, with lab; 2.5 years of chemistry, some with labs; some calculus and possibly some statistics; and a variety of biology courses. The remainder of undergraduate courses would be in disciplines outside of the sciences. A study of the "core" or required biology courses for undergraduate biology majors was carried out by Dominick Marocco . He states that required courses reveal "the consensus of the faculty at an institution that the subject matter of the core is central to the education of a biologist." He concludes that a consensus core based on the requirements at the 104 schools surveyed would include genetics, biochemistry, cell biology, microbiology, evolution/ecology, and a seminar. Another major impact on today's curriculum are requirements for admission to medical school. This issue is discussed further in Recommendation #7, found in Chapter 6.

The physical sciences and mathematics background of biology majors can best be strengthened by integrated teaching rather than by the addition of courses taught in isolation of biology. Though all of the topics found on the concept lists are offered in most universities and colleges, it is difficult for life science students to master the essential ones without taking a larger number of courses than can be accommodated in a biology major. Hence, the committee recommends the creation of new courses (or revamping of old courses) to cover the most pertinent part of this material in less time and with examples geared toward biology. Furthermore, as with key concepts in the physical sciences that are relevant for the study of biological systems, biology faculty can further enhance students' understanding of the connections between mathematics, computer science, and biology by introducing these concepts into courses in the biology curriculum. Relevant courses might be taught by faculty from mathematics, computer science, or biology, or by a collaborating team of faculty from multiple departments. Outside input should be sought if the course is to be taught by a biologist who does not have extensive interdisciplinary experience. A mathematician or computer scientist might also be invited to give a guest lecture or two. Similarly, biologists should provide assistance to the mathematics and computer science faculty in designing biological examples for use in their courses.

One aspect of reform is the reevaluation of the topics covered in introductory courses. Is some material covered just because it is in the textbook or has "traditionally" been taught in this course? Are there other topics that would be more useful or more relevant or interesting to the students currently enrolled in the course? By adding modules and redesigning courses, a department can make its curriculum more interdisciplinary without any increase in the number of courses required.

The order in which the material is taught should be carefully considered in relation to the rest of the curriculum. For example, the early introduction of statistics and discrete mathematics could be beneficial for biology courses. This is the type of change that should be assessed after implementation to see if it is beneficial to student learning. While a substantial part of the material in the concept lists can be taught as mathematics, chemistry, or physics (with biological examples), some of the more advanced and more specifically biological material might instead be covered in a biology course or an interdepartmental course, depending on the teaching resources and interests of the particular departments. For example, a course on modeling could be taught in many different departments, or modules on modeling could be added to preexisting courses. Those biology students who wish to eventually work at the interface of biology and physical, mathematical or information sciences will need to become more expert in those fields, and may want to take some of the standard courses offered in those disciplines that provide a more rigorous foundation. The integration of disciplines may also be well served through the development of an interdisciplinary concentration in mathematics or physics, so that biology and other faculty and departments can work more closely together, through shared resources and curriculum, to develop and maintain a program that is best tailored to address student needs.

In the traditional program, a full year of general chemistry is followed by a full year of organic chemistry, and then by physical chemistry. Some institutions are now adopting nontraditional plans, in which organic chemistry is taught earlier. Several have experimented with organic chemistry as the first course; for biology students, the advantage is they can start studying biochemistry in their second year with the chemical background needed to understand it. Earlier knowledge of biochemistry is useful in many biology courses, ranging from genetics to development. Another way to allow students to learn biochemistry earlier is to restructure the introductory chemistry course so that only one semester is required before students begin organic chemistry. This plan is well suited to biology majors who can take both general chemistry and half of organic chemistry in their first year, preparing them for chemistry-based biology in their second year. One-semester courses to follow organic chemistry could include concepts of physical chemistry, perhaps focusing on solution chemistry; an introduction to analytical chemistry; or biochemistry at a chemically sophisticated level (i.e., where biomolecular structure and reaction mechanisms are presented in considerable depth). Relevant biological examples should be part of these courses, and indeed part of the organic and general chemistry courses as well.

Restructuring chemistry courses along these lines would be compatible with the needs of physicists, geologists, and nonchemical engineers who often need to take one year of chemistry. A yearlong course covering both inorganic and organic chemistry would also be useful for humanities and social science students seeking an overview of chemistry to meet their science requirements. It would be more demanding than many of the courses currently offered to nonscience majors, but potentially more appealing because of its increased use of applied examples that students are more easily able to relate to their own lives and surroundings. A first semester of organic chemistry, given in the spring, could include a general survey of the properties of the major classes of organic compounds and their key reactions, so those students not going further in chemistry would still have a reasonable picture of the subject. A second semester of organic chemistry, given in the fall of the second year for chemists, biologists, and chemical engineers, could then be a more advanced treatment, with more information on mechanism and synthesis than in the first semester.

The typical two-semester introductory physics course with calculus, which has changed rather little over more than a quarter-century, is often the only option for a biology student who wants a strong physics preparation. One way to teach the material on the physics concept list, described earlier in the chapter, would be as a three-semester sequence. However, there are other ways that such material could be covered. For example, the more conventional physics topics might be covered by a one-year course within a physics department while the other materials (which more specifically bridge biology and physics) might then be part of another course, in either the physics or biology department; in fact, some of it is appropriate for a physical chemistry course. The choice of department and number of semesters would vary from institution to institution, and depend to some degree on the expertise of the faculty in each department. Alternatively the material could be taught as an interdepartmental course. While all the topics listed have direct relevance to biology, the emphasis in course design should be on learning and developing the relationship between observations and mathematical description and modeling, rather than on slavishly covering every topic.

An attractive option for quantitative literacy, mathematics, and computer science at some institutions might be the development of an integrated course to teach quantitative approaches and tools for research, as has been successfully developed at the University of Tennessee (see Case Study #4.) This innovative two-semester course designed for life science majors replaces the traditional calculus course. It introduces topics such as the mathematics of discrete variables, linear algebra, statistics, programming, and modeling early in the course, to provide completely new material for well-prepared students. These topics are then connected to applied aspects of calculus. It should be noted that this course makes extensive use of graduate students in Tennessee's mathematical and computational ecology program. These graduate students are well positioned to explain the connections between mathematics and biology.

A two-semester quantitative course such as the one at Tennessee exposes students to many mathematical ideas but is too brief to provide much depth in many of them. A more intensive alternative would be a four-semester series. Two semesters could deal with calculus (single and multivariate), quantitative differential equations (including phase plane analysis), and the relevant elementary linear algebra, taught in the context of biological applications. A third semester might be on biostatistics, emphasizing different ways to analyze and interpret data. A fourth semester could include discrete math and algorithms and could be taught in the context of biological issues, including those arising in genomics.

In summary, for the future biomedical researcher, the committee proposes:

• A reorganization of the chemistry offerings to allow for the early presentation of organic chemistry and the addition of some analytical and physical chemistry to the organic and inorganic courses. One potential arrangement of courses would be for students to start with a one-semester introductory inorganic course (rather than the two currently taught at many institutions), followed by two semesters of organic, one (or two) of biochemistry and then a combined physical and analytical course.

• An expansion of the physics offerings to include a third semester that incorporates engineering principles into the syllabus in order to assist students in becoming familiar with modeling and analysis of biological and other systems.   Other topics might include molecular physics, biospectroscopies, and dynamical networks.

• A new mathematics sequence that exposes students to statistics, probability, discrete math, linear algebra, calculus, and modeling without requiring that a full semester be spent on each topic. A brief overview of these topics could be presented in two semesters, but a full introduction and the inclusion of more computer science would more likely take four semesters.

Potential Curricula

Four quite different examples of a modernized four-year curriculum for a biology major are presented below to stimulate discussion among faculty. These tables represent various course options a student might take. They do not represent proposed requirements for a major. At first glance the courses in the tables may not look so different from the current offerings at some colleges. The idea here is to incorporate some of the concepts presented earlier in the chapter into each of these science courses. Another change from the current practice at some universities would be the increased incorporation of teaching techniques such as inquiry-based learning and approaches such as those presented in the next two chapters. Many institutions would need to revamp their course offerings in order to allow their students to create this type of course mix. A student taking all the courses listed in one of the following examples would likely exceed the institution's requirements for a biology major. Different choices will be made by different schools and different students. For example, the content of mathematics courses may be influenced by the types of material covered in that school's biology courses. Opportunities to learn mathematical skills in a rich content context will enhance conceptual understanding and procedural fluency.

The committee envisions two levels of potential changes that could facilitate interdisciplinary learning. In the first level of change, the goal would be on increasing communication between science departments and working together to develop and integrate modules into preexisting courses. The following chapters of the report present some examples of potential modules that could be used to provide students with real-world examples of how mathematics, chemistry, physics, computer science, and engineering are useful in the study of biology. In the second level of change, interdisciplinary courses could be developed (possibly using team teaching approaches) or biology-focused science or mathematics courses could be developed. The committee recognizes that it may be difficult for some schools, particularly small ones, to add new courses unless they replace preexisting course offerings. However, these same schools may have other advantages, such as a small science faculty that is used to working with colleagues outside their own immediate area of specialization that would facilitate the creation of modules or increase the feasibility of team teaching.

Some aspects of curriculum A are more complex than can be represented in the table that follows: The yearlong mathematics sequence suggested for first-year students could be a newly designed course modeled after Case Study #4 taught at the University of Tennessee, or one that covers selected aspects of calculus, differential equations, linear algebra, and statistics. At some schools, students will continue to take traditional mathematics courses. For some of those students, calculus would be appropriate, others will need remedial mathematics courses, still others will enter with calculus and might enroll in discrete math and/or computer science courses. For more ideas, see Appendix F: Mathematics and Computer Science Panel Summary. Possible biology electives (for the senior year) include Bioinformatics and Computational Biology, Mechanics of Organisms (see Case Study #5), Organismal Physiology, Comparative or Human Anatomy, Toxicology, Neurobiology, and Environmental Biochemistry. At

Potential Curriculum A

	Fall	Spring
First year	Introductory Biology I (and lab)	Introductory Biology II (and lab)
	Inorganic Chemistry (and lab)	Organic Chemistry I (and lab)
	Introductory Math I[a]	Introductory Math II
		Faculty Research Seminar
	General Education Elective	General Education Elective
	General Education Elective	
Sophomore	Molecular Biology	Cell and Developmental Biology
	Organic Chemistry II (and lab)	Biochemistry
	Introductory Physics I (and lab)	Introductory Physics II
		(and Engineering lab)
	General Education Elective	
	General Education Elective	General Education Elective
		General Education Elective
Junior	Analytical/Physical Chemistry	Evolutionary Biology/Ecology
	(and lab)	Biology Laboratory Course
	Genetics	
	General Education Elective	General Education Elective
	General Education Elective	General Education Elective
	Independent Laboratory Research	Independent Laboratory Research
Senior	Biology Elective	Biology Elective
	Science Elective	Science Elective
		Faculty Research Seminar
	General Education Elective	General Education Elective
	General Education Elective	
	Independent Laboratory Research	Independent Laboratory Research

[a]For more ideas, see Appendix F: Mathematics and Computer Science Panel Summary.

Potential Curriculum B

	Fall	Spring
First year	Introductory Biology I (and lab) Inorganic Chemistry (and lab) Introductory Math I	Introductory Biology II (and lab) Probability and BioStatistics Introductory Math II Faculty Research Seminar
	General Education Elective General Education Elective	General Education Elective
Sophomore	Molecular Biology Differential Equations Introductory Physics I (and lab)	Cell and Developmental Biology Organic Chemistry I (and lab) Physics II (and Engineering lab)
	General Education Elective General Education Elective	General Education Elective General Education Elective
Junior	Genetics Organic Chemistry II (and lab) Physics III (and Engineering lab)	Evolutionary Biology/Ecology Biology Laboratory Course Biochemistry
	General Education Elective	General Education Elective
	Independent Laboratory Research	Independent Laboratory Research
Senior	Biology Elective Science/Biology Elective Analytical/Physical Chemistry (and lab)	Advanced Mathematics (e.g., discrete math that builds on genetics already learned) Science/Biology Elective Faculty Research Seminar
	General Education Elective	General Education Elective
	Independent Laboratory Research	Independent Laboratory Research

least some of the upper-level biology courses should include labs. For example, students might take a lab along with genetics, molecular biology, or biochemistry, but not necessarily with all three courses.

Alternatively, a more quantitative track could be designed as an option for students who are interested in exploring the interfaces between biology, mathematics, computer science, and the physical sciences (Curriculum B).

A more radical change in undergraduate biology proposal appears as Potential Curriculum C below. The key idea is that contemporary biology cannot be taught effectively until students have a sufficiently strong background in chemistry, physics, math, and computer science. Consequently, biology is not taught in the first year, apart from a seminar designed to whet the appetite of students for biological research and stimulate their acquisition of a strong background in the physical sciences. Rather, the first year is devoted to providing students with the requisite background in the physical sciences and mathematics.

It is difficult to teach chemistry, physics, math, and computer science all in the first year. To succeed, the content of these courses has to be quite different from that of traditional courses in these areas. Also, the notion that an introductory course must occupy two semesters in the same academic year would have to be put aside. The primary objective of the first year would be to provide students with the physical science knowledge and tools needed to effectively study biology starting in the second year at a level that prepares them for contemporary biological research as it is being carried out today. In the proposed curriculum, Chemistry I and II would introduce students to inorganic chemistry, organic chemistry, and key aspects of biomolecular interactions. Math I would deal with differential calculus and elementary linear algebra, and Math II with integral calculus, probability, and statistics. Computer Science I would teach algorithms, simulation of dynamical systems, string (sequence) comparisons, and clustering; a high-level language such as Matlab or Mathematica would be used. Physics I would present mechanics, followed by equilibrium statistical physics. Waves, electrostatics, and collective phenomena would be presented in Physics II, followed by signal analysis and processing, basic quantum mechanics, and spectroscopy in Physics III.

The four-semester core biology sequence (Molecular Biology, Cell and Developmental Biology, Genetics, and Evolutionary Biology/Ecology) starting in the sophomore year could be taught with a quantitative emphasis that would draw more heavily than now on the physical sciences, mathematics, and computer science. For example, emergent system properties at

Potential Curriculum C

	Fall	Spring
First year	Biology Seminar	Physics I (and lab)
	Chemistry I (and lab)	Chemistry II (and lab)
	Math I[a]	Computer Science I
	General Education Elective	General Education Elective
	General Education Elective	General Education Elective
Sophomore	Molecular Biology	Cell and Developmental Biology
	Math II	Biophysical Chemistry
	Physics II (and lab)	Physics III (and Engineering lab)
	General Education Elective	General Education Elective
	General Education Elective	General Education Elective
Junior	Genetics	Evolutionary Biology/Ecology
	Biochemistry	Biology Laboratory Course
	Biology Elective	
		General Education Elective
	General Education Elective	General Education Elective
	Independent Laboratory Research	Independent Laboratory Research
Senior	Biology Elective	Math or Computer Science
	Chemistry Elective	Elective
		Science/Biology Elective
	General Education Elective	Faculty Research Seminar
	General Education Elective	
		General Education Elective
	Independent Laboratory Research	Independent Laboratory Research

[a]For more ideas, see Appendix F: Mathematics and Computer Science Panel Summary.

Potential Curriculum D

	Fall	Spring
First year	Introductory Biology I (and lab)	Introductory Biology II (and lab)
	Inorganic Chemistry (and lab)	Organic/Biochemistry I (and lab)
	Calculus and Differential Equations I	Calculus and Differential Equations II
	General Education Elective	Faculty Research Seminar
	General Education Elective	General Education Elective
Sophomore	Molecular Biology	Cell and Developmental Biology
	Organic/Biochemistry II (and lab)	Biostatistics
	Introductory Physics I (and lab)	Introductory Physics II (and lab)
	General Education Elective	General Education Elective
	General Education Elective	General Education Elective
Junior	Genetics (and lab)	Evolutionary Biology
	Computer Science	Biology Laboratory Course
	General Education Elective	General Education Elective
	General Education Elective	General Education Elective
	Independent Laboratory Research	Independent Laboratory Research
Senior	Biology Elective	Biology Elective
	Science Elective	Science Elective
		Faculty Research Seminar
	General Education Elective	
	General Education Elective	General Education Elective
	Independent Laboratory Research	Independent Laboratory Research

all levels of biological organization (e.g., in signal transduction cascades, genetic regulatory circuits, and ecosystems) could be taught making extensive use of quantitative models.

The fourth potential curriculum is intended for students who are especially interested in evolution, ecology, and systematics. It assumes students enter already having taken calculus and calls for specific courses in biostatistics and computer science, essential tools for the study of evolution. Students focusing on evolution may go on to pursue many types of activities, ranging from field research to clinical research. As discussed earlier, the connections between different types of biology are growing stronger just as the connections between different sciences are growing.

Biology is an increasingly complex science that is truly an integrative discipline in which many aspects of mathematics and physical science converge to address biological issues. For biology majors to receive an optimal education, the content of their curriculum must be updated to address the interdisciplinary nature of the field. At many institutions, this will mean changes in the course offerings so that those who will become future biomedical researchers learn more mathematics and more physical and information sciences than is currently required. It continues to make sense for biology majors to take introductory courses in chemistry and physics and to enroll in courses in the mathematics department. However, for this practice to be most useful, the students must learn how to relate the material they learn in those courses to biology and how to relate the material they learn in biology courses to chemistry and physics. Perhaps of equal importance, students majoring in mathematics and physical sciences should learn how to relate the material they learn to issues of biology.

The recommendations of this report will not be achieved solely by transforming an undergraduate's schedule into one of the curricular examples shown above. However, much can be accomplished without altering the current list of course titles. The content of the courses must change to incorporate the concepts presented in the first half of this chapter. Different schools will likely create different sets of courses. Incorporating these themes into biology courses and ensuring that they are covered in other science courses taken by biologists will greatly benefit the education of biology majors, as well as, the committee believes, other undergraduates who are enrolled in these courses.

3

Instructional Materials and Approaches for Interdisciplinary Teaching

RECOMMENDATION #3

Successful interdisciplinary teaching will require new materials and approaches. College and university administrators, as well as funding agencies, should support mathematics and science faculty in the development or adaptation of techniques that improve interdisciplinary education for biologists. These techniques would include courses, modules (on biological problems suitable for study in mathematics and physical science courses and vice versa), and other teaching materials. These endeavors are time-consuming and difficult and will require serious financial support. In addition, for truly interdisciplinary education to be achieved, administrative and financial barriers to cross-departmental collaboration between faculty must be eliminated.

Outstanding textbooks such as Linus Pauling's *General Chemistry* and James Watson's *Molecular Biology of the Gene* have enriched and transformed undergraduate education in the past. These innovative works defined new areas of science and made them accessible and exciting to future scientists at a crucial formative stage. The need for works that sculpt science in ways that inform, enlighten, and empower the next generation of researchers is even greater today. First, new architectures that encompass the highly interdisciplinary character of biology can accelerate the learning process and enable students to exercise their talents earlier in their careers. Second, new technologies provide exceptional opportunities for enhancing the learning process. The potentialities of computers and computer graphics have barely been tapped. They need to be integrated into traditional teaching and developed as distinctive media that stand on their own. This chapter highlights some opportunities, starting with interdisciplinary modules.

The physical science and mathematics background of life science majors should be markedly strengthened by bringing principles and examples drawn from these disciplines into the teaching of biology courses. No longer should these disciplines be regarded merely as courses to be "taken" by life science students. Rather, they should be woven into the teaching of biology itself to better illustrate the integrative and interdisciplinary nature of the life sciences. The next section presents examples of ways to integrate two or more sciences together into one course. The ideas presented here may be helpful in designing courses for the curricular ideas and arrangements presented in Chapter 2.

MODULES FOR COURSE ENRICHMENT

The purpose of this section is to provide some of the best examples identified in the course of this study as models for faculty who may want to incorporate some of the ideas into their own teaching. A step toward interdisciplinary teaching can be taken by using modules that focus on important principles of mathematics and the physical and information sciences in order to demonstrate their relevance to biology. A module could be presented in a single lecture or laboratory session, or over several sessions. For example, a module on allosteric interactions in hemoglobin could enrich the teaching of respiratory physiology. Students could explore the following questions by carrying out interactive computer simulations: How does the cooperative binding of oxygen to hemoglobin increase the efficiency of oxygen transport? How much oxygen is released from hemoglobin when the pH is lowered? How is oxygen transport affected by high altitude?

Modules have been developed and integrated into science curricula with success at some institutions, but this approach has not been widely adopted at a majority of institutions nationwide. The use of biological examples as modules in courses on chemistry, physics, computer science, and mathematics could help make those courses more relevant to future biological research scientists. Well-chosen examples that vividly present the biological pertinence of the physical or mathematical concepts under study can help students draw connections between material taught in different courses. Faculty from different disciplines should get together to prepare a series of interdisciplinary modules and associated teaching materials such as computer simulations and animations. Several examples of topics in biology that could be effectively taught using modules that present concepts from mathematics and the physical and information sciences are given at the end of this section. The mathematics, physics, chemistry, or engineering background needed for each module could be succinctly developed in the context of a biological question.

Adaptable modules for course enrichment that take full advantage of interactive computer programs and multimedia educational tools are a very attractive complementary means of strengthening undergraduate biology education. They can be designed for class use or independent study. Highly focused modules conveying connections between disciplines could be presented in a single teaching session or over several days depending on their scope and their role in the course. The NSF has launched the National Science Digital Library (*http://www.smete.org/*) as a gathering place for resources in science education. The idea is to provide a virtual gathering spot, a peer-reviewed library on education, and tested resources for teaching science. The NSDL is being assembled in parts. An example of a fully functioning component is the library for earth system education (*http://www.dlese.org/*). The biology component, BioSciEdNet (BEN), is still under development (*www.biosciednet.org/*), but could be a valuable resource if the community embraces it.

Numerous independent groups have published modules or resources that could be used to enhance the teaching of undergraduate biology students. One group that has developed numerous modules for biology courses and laboratories is the BioQUEST Curriculum Consortium (Case Study #2). Examples of problem-based learning can be found at the University of Delaware's clearinghouse (*http://www.udel.edu/pbl/*). Case studies are collected by the National Center for Case Study Teaching in Science at SUNY Buffalo (*http://ublib.buffalo.edu/libraries/projects/cases/case.html*). The Consortium for Mathematics and its Applications has a project, Intermath, that works to foster the creation of interdisciplinary courses that demonstrate the interdependence of mathematics and science. They have produced supplementary modules in a searchable database at *http://www.comap.com/undergraduate/* and also publish *The UMAP Journal.*

A sample module is presented here (Case Study #3); it was designed for a course in organic chemistry. The premise of the module is that studying the infectivity of the influenza virus is an effective means of engaging student interest in carbohydrates and teaching principles of molecular recognition and rational drug design in a stimulating context.

CASE STUDY #2
BioQUEST Curriculum Consortium

BioQUEST designs, develops, and publishes teaching materials to support investigative, student-centered learning. The BioQUEST Library is a peer-reviewed publication of computer-based curricular materials for biology education. The current volume (VI) contains more than 75 software simulations and supporting materials from diverse areas of biology, such as Biota (modeling and simulating population dynamics), *Evolve* (population genetics), Isolated Heart Laboratory (pressure-volume relationships in a variety of physiological states), Epidemiology (simulation of the spread of an infectious disease), and Diffusion Laboratories (models of pattern formation in development). These modules include quantitative approaches to the study topics.

The consortium also provides opportunities for faculty development in the form of nine-day summer workshops at Beloit College. For example, one BioQUEST Curriculum summer workshop focused on change in introductory biology courses. Participants had the opportunity to experience, as a student would, the use of research strategies to pose and explore biological problems. These investigations were built around the use of several BioQUEST modules including Genetics Construction Kit, Environmental Decision Making, BIRRD, Demography, EcoBeaker, Evolve, Wading Bird, and others. Materials developed collaboratively, such as LifeLines Online cases and bioinformatics problems from the Workbench Users' group, were also featured. Their co-developed curriculum materials also include an Internet-based suite of bioinformatics tools and databases, a database and tools for exploring evolution via multiple data resources, investigative cases for introductory biology in two-year institutions, and multimedia resources for the American Society for Microbiology video series *Unseen Life on Earth.*

For more information: *http://bioquest.org*

CASE STUDY #3
Carbohydrates in Organic Chemistry

In his organic chemistry course Jerry Mohrig integrates material on carbohydrates by having a capstone to his yearlong course. This capstone is called "Why do we get the flu every year?" It treats the basic chemistry of carbohydrates, proteins, and molecular recognition in a modern context, and it provides a story line that runs through the whole course. Information on glycobiology, molecular recognition, and cell-cell interactions is integrated throughout both semesters as a story line. Originally, he tried to use multiple isolated biological examples, but the relevance did not connect for the students. This example about the flu was chosen instead of details on how egg and sperm bind because more is known about the viral system.

Although the basics of carbohydrate and amino acid chemistry are taught as part of most second-term organic chemistry courses, many students would be hard pressed to recognize or appreciate the great importance that carbohydrates have in biochemical recognition. The structures of oligosaccharides and their binding to protein recognition sites are straightforward enough to teach in the second-semester organic course. The flu module focuses on the recognition by the influenza virus of two crucial proteins with sialic acid units attached to cell surfaces. The viral hemagglutinin binds to neuraminic acid residues on the surface of the respiratory tract and the viral neuraminidase cleaves these residues. The interactions allow viral invasion of cells, and understanding these interac-

Some other ideas for modules to enrich the teaching of biology include the following:

- *What determines whether an epidemic waxes or wanes?* In a simple model, a population consists of susceptibles who can contract a disease, infectives who can transmit it, and removals who have had the disease and are neither susceptible nor infective. Given an infection rate, a removal rate, and initial sizes of the three groups, one can calculate how the population evolves. Mathematical treatments, illuminated by examples of plague, flu, and AIDS epidemics, are given by Murray (1993, pp. 610-696) and by Hoppensteadt and Peskin (1992, pp. 67-81).

tions has also led to the development of neuraminidase inhalators that serve as therapeutic agents. The module ends with the neuraminidase inhibitors that are available to fight flu symptoms. One question on the final exam is an x-ray picture of a monosaccharide bound to a protein recognition site. The students are asked to describe the noncovalent interactions that are responsible for the binding.

Dr. Mohrig believes that it is not enough to teach future biologists the organic chemistry of small molecules if they never see how this knowledge can be applied to biological molecules of consequence. It is important that students see that they can make sense of how to relate complex organic molecules to biological questions and develop the confidence to do so. Since he has been teaching the flu module, he has seen a significant increase in the interest in organic chemistry of the many biology students in the course. He also designed a carry-forward questionnaire on the value of the module to students who subsequently enroll in an immunology course. He asked students one or two years after the flu example to answer a question on immunological aspects of influenza. Student opinion on the value of the module increased if they later took a biology course in which the professor discussed the chemistry of carbohydrates. The biology faculty had to communicate to their students that chemistry was essential to fully understand the biological system.

For more information: *http://mc2.cchem.berkeley.edu/modules/flu/*

• *What accounts for the all-or-none character of nerve action potentials?* The classic Hodgin-Huxley model of action potentials is presented by Hille (2001, pp. 45-60). A module on the Hodgkin-Huxley model of nerve action potentials would deepen students' understanding of how information is transmitted over long distances in the nervous system. Students can explore the following questions by carrying out interactive computer simulations: What gives rise to the all-or-none nature of action potentials? What accounts for the threshold in generating action potentials? What factors govern their frequency? The molecular properties of two kinds of channels account for this fundamental signaling process. The interplay of cooperativity, positive feedback, deactivation, and delayed reactivation can be vividly demonstrated by interactive simulations. For more information: *http://pb010.anes.ucla.edu/nervelt/nervelt.html*

• *How can chance events markedly alter gene frequencies in small populations?* Consider an allele initially present at a frequency of 0.5. As was shown by Kimura, the allele will, on average, become fixed or lost after 2.77 N generations, where N is the population size. Genetic drift is akin to diffusion, as discussed by Hartl and Clark (1997, pp. 267-313).

• *How do leopards get their spots and zebras get their stripes?* In 1952, Alan Turing published a seminal paper showing that an initially homogeneous distribution of chemicals can give rise to heterogeneous spatial patterns by reaction and diffusion. Animal coat patterns and other applications of reaction diffusion mechanisms are discussed by Murray (1993, pp. 434-480)

• *How can topology and knot theory help us understand the packing of DNA in the cell nucleus?* DNA can be visualized as a complicated knot that must be unknotted by enzymes in order for replication or transcription to occur. A mathematical knot is a closed curve. This can be visualized as a closed loop of string. If the string had a knot in it, it would be impossible to unknot without slicing through the loop. This analogy can help students understand the actions of topoisomerase enzymes on DNA. For more information: *http://www.tiem.utk.edu/~harrell/webmodules/DNAknot.html*

• *Exploring the Nanoworld.* Vivid explorations of many facets of materials at the nanoscale can be made at the Exploring the Nanoworld Web site. LEGOÒ bricks are used to build models demonstrating pertinent physical and chemical principles. This site also demonstrates how a laser pointer and an optical transform slide can be used to show how Watson and Crick deduced that DNA is double helical. For more information: *http://mrsec.wisc.edu/edetc/*

INTERDISCIPLINARY LECTURE AND SEMINAR COURSES

In addition to modules, interdisciplinary lecture and seminar courses can give students a better and more realistic picture of how connections between different areas of science are made in research. Because research is becoming increasingly interdisciplinary, such courses should be made available to students beginning in their first year. There are several possible formats for courses that extensively combine the teaching of physical sciences, mathematics, and/or engineering with the teaching of life sciences. One example is presented in Case Study #4. Such courses could be presented at various times during undergraduate study. The courses could be distinguished by purpose and the number of prerequisites.

At one end of the spectrum could be a truly interdisciplinary course used as an introductory first-year seminar with relatively few details and no prerequisites. It could serve as a "whet the appetite" course to introduce students to many disciplines in their first year, and to hold the interest of first-year students who are taking disciplinary prerequisites prior to starting courses in biological sciences. This course could have a single theme; an example of a first-year seminar on plagues that draws on different disciplines is described in Case Study #11. An alternative format could feature a series of faculty or guest speakers who present case studies on a wide range of topics exemplified by genomics, environmental science, infectious disease epidemiology, medical statistics, computational biology, mathematical biology, toxicology, and risk assessment. Such a course would serve a dual role: biology students would see that mathematics and computation play an important role in their future work, and mathematics and computer science students would get a taste of how quantitative methods (statistics, applied mathematics, computer science) can be fruitfully applied in biology and medicine.

At the other end of the spectrum could be a capstone course for seniors with substantial educational experience in multiple disciplines. With extensive prerequisites in these disciplines, an interdisciplinary course organized around a topic could be presented at an advanced level. On the Mechanics of Organisms, an upper-level course at the University of California at Berkeley, effectively brings biology and engineering together (Case Study #5). Engineering principles pertinent to particular biological processes are presented first, followed by their place in biology. This is only one example, and many other upper-level courses can be imagined that would vividly illustrate the interplay of biology with the physical and mathematical sciences and engineering, such as Three-dimensional Structure Determination (x-ray diffraction, nuclear magnetic resonance spectroscopy), Sensory Signaling Systems (vision, smell, taste, hearing, and touch), Biological Imaging (fluorescence microscopy, confocal imaging, evanescent wave microscopy, two-photon imaging), and Medical Imaging (functional magnetic resonance imaging, positron emission tomography, ultrasound).

At intermediate levels, a variety of course plans could incorporate material from the physical sciences, and the mathematical concepts and skills that subtend these disciplines, into biological courses. Possible examples are a course in quantitative physiology (blood circulation, gas exchange in the

CASE STUDY #4
Quantitative Education for Biologists
University of Tennessee

This course sequence provides an introduction to a variety of mathematical topics of use in analyzing problems arising in the biological sciences. It is designed for students in biology, agriculture, forestry, wildlife, and premedicine and other prehealth professions. The general aim of the sequence is to show how mathematical and analytical tools may be used to explore and explain a wide variety of biological phenomena that are not easily understood with verbal reasoning alone.

Prerequisites are two years of high school algebra, one year of geometry, and half a year of trigonometry. The goals of the course are to develop the students' ability to quantitatively analyze problems arising in their own work in biology, to illustrate the great utility of mathematical models to provide answers to key biological problems, and to provide experience using computer software to analyze data and investigate mathematical models. This is accomplished by encouraging hypothesis formulation and testing and the investigation of real-world biological problems through the use of data. Another goal is to reduce rote memorization of mathematical formulae and rules through the use of software including Matlab and MicroCalc. Students can be encouraged to investigate biological areas of particular interest to them using a variety of quantitative software from a diversity of biological specialties.

In many respects, this course is more difficult than the university's science/engineering calculus sequence (Math 141-142) since it covers a wider variety of mathematical topics, is coupled to real data, and involves the use of the computer. Although the course is challenging, it has been designed specifically for life science students, and includes many more biological examples than other mathematics courses. It, therefore, introduces the students to quantitative concepts not covered in these other math courses that they should find useful in their biology courses. The main text is *Mathematics for the Biosciences* by Michael Cullen, which is extensively supplemented by material provided in class.

Each class session begins with the students generating one or more hypotheses regarding a biological or mathematical topic germane to that day's material. For example, students go outdoors to collect leaf size data. They are then asked: Are leaf width and length related? Is the relationship the same for all tree species? What affects leaf sizes? Why do some trees have larger leaves

CASE STUDY #4 CONTINUED

than others? Each of these questions could generate many hypotheses, and students can then go on to use Matlab to analyze the data sets they collect in order to evaluate the hypotheses. Some hypotheses do not relate to a biological area and are based on mathematics alone. For example, after linear regression is introduced, students are asked whether this regression can be reasonably used to determine the y-value for an x-value for which there are no data. This leads naturally to a discussion of interpolation and extrapolation.

As each topic is introduced, the instructor includes a brief description of how it relates to biology. This is often done by having a background biological example used for each main mathematical topic being covered, which can be referred to regularly as the math is developed. For example, in covering matrices, the material can be introduced with this example: "Suppose you are a land manager in the U.S. West, and you have satellite images of the land you manage taken every year for several years. The images clearly show whether a point on the image (actually a 500 m x 500 m plot of land) is bare soil, grassland, or shrubland. How can you use these to help you manage the system?" From this, the students develop the key notion of a transition matrix; the professor can then go on to matrix multiplication, and eigenvalues and eigenvectors for describing dynamics of the landscape and the long-term fraction in bare soil, grass, and shrubs.

Attempts are made to include real, rather than fabricated, data in class demonstrations, project assignments, and exams. For example, data of monthly CO_2 concentrations in the Northern Hemisphere can be used to introduce semi-log regression, and allometry data can be used for studying log-log regressions. Students are encouraged to collect their own data for appropriate portions of the course, particularly the descriptive statistics section. Scientific journal articles that use the math under study are also provided.

Syllabus Math 151:

Descriptive statistics—analysis of tabular data, means, variances, histograms, linear regression

Exponentials and logarithms, non-linear scalings, allometry

Matrix algebra—addition, subtraction, multiplication, inverses, matrix models in population biology, eigenvalues, eigenvectors, Markov chains, ecological succession

Discrete probability—population genetics, behavioral sequence analysis

Sequences and difference equations—introduction to sequences and limit concept

Syllabus Math 152:
Difference equations, linear and nonlinear examples, equilibrium, stability and homeostasis, logistic models, introduction to limits
Limits of functions and continuity
Derivatives and curve sketching
Exponential and logarithms
Antiderivatives and integrals
Trigonometric functions
Differential equations and modeling

Students are graded through weekly 10-minute quizzes, assignments based on the use of the computer to analyze particular sets of data or problems (some done in groups), three in-class exams, and a comprehensive final exam. The exams are generally not computer-based, focusing rather on the key concepts and techniques discussed in the course. Extra-credit opportunities require students to evaluate one of a wide variety of software programs available involving some area of biology. This requires becoming very familiar with the program, and writing a formal review of the software, in the same format as might appear in a scientific journal.

For more information: *http://www.tiem.utk.edu/~gross/ quant.lifesci.html*

lung, control of cell volume, electrical activity of neurons, renal countercurrent mechanism, muscle mechanics) or a course in population biology (epidemic and endemic disease, ecological dynamics, population genetics, evolution). Such interdisciplinary courses could provide excellent opportunities to learn important mathematical skills, such as deriving equations, using computer simulations, and working in teams. Many topics could be taught at an elementary or more advanced level, depending on the ways in which the mathematics is treated. For example, ordinary differential equations can be made tractable via Euler's method without the need for a for-

CASE STUDY #5
Seminar on the Mechanics of Organisms
University of California at Berkeley

This upper-level interdisciplinary course brings biology and engineering together. It teaches functional morphology in terms of mechanical design principles. The basics of fluid and solid mechanics are covered along with examples of their biological implications, stressing the dependence of mechanical behavior on the structure of molecules, tissues, structural elements, whole organisms, and habitats.

Organisms are introduced as "Living Machines" and their abilities to fly, swim, parachute, glide, walk, run, buckle, twist, and stretch are evaluated in the context of physics and engineering principles. Students learn about the different types of fluid flow (laminar, tubular, large and small scale), the fluid dynamic forces of drag and lift, and how organisms live on wave-swept shores. They consider other biological issues such as life at low Reynolds number (the sticky world of small organisms), benthic boundary layers and flow microhabitats, and fluid dynamics of filters including suspension feeding. They evaluate stress distribution in structures, including tension, compression, shear, beam theory, buckling, twisting, kinking, and strain. They learn about the biomechanics of bone, muscle, and cells, and the idea of molecular motors. They consider issues of size and scaling of organisms, how mechanical properties change during the life of an organism, the physics of shape changes in morphogenesis, viscoelasticity, resilience and plasticity, as well as fracture and the evolution of safety features.

For more information: *http://ib.berkeley.edu/about.html*

mal background in differential equations. Euler's method provides a simplified method for obtaining an approximate numerical solution to a differential equation. Simulations involving random numbers can be done with only an intuitive introduction to probability and the use of a random number generator. A computer language such as Matlab makes it easy to write programs that implement Euler's method (and other similar methods), and also provides easy access to graphical output, including animations.

TEACHING MATERIALS

Making biology education more interdisciplinary and representative of how biological research is actually conducted is critically dependent on the availability of new and innovative teaching materials. Teaching materials are not solely textbooks; they also include computer-based materials, instructor guides, modules, and case studies. Textbooks that bridge different disciplines and provide a coherent framework for study and learning can play a vital role in achieving the objective of more interdisciplinary and relevant biology education. Many high-quality biology textbooks are available, but publishers could do more. For example, it is especially rare to find detailed mention of physical science or mathematical principles in introductory biology texts. The committee is not aware of any comparative analysis of biology textbooks for the college level; however, two different groups, the American Association for the Advancement of Science and the American Institute of Biological Sciences, have evaluated biology textbooks used in high schools. Both groups conclude that the books provide massive quantities of information, which may result in sacrificing depth and conceptual understanding as teachers attempt to cover the material (*http://www.project2061.org/newsinfo/research/textbook/hsbio/about.htm*) Some of the suggestions made in these reports may prove useful to those writing or revising college textbooks.

Representative texts that emphasize interdisciplinary aspects of science are given in the box at the end of the chapter.[1] Although the list is not comprehensive, many more are needed. In selecting these titles, the committee looked for books that drew connections between multiple scientific disciplines. Although not all the books listed reflect recent scientific advances, they do illustrate exemplary approaches to their topics. Educational institutions, professional societies, private and public foundations, and publishers should work together to ensure that interdisciplinary materials are produced. The National Institute for Science Education's College Level One team at the University of Wisconsin-Madison has been active in developing teaching materials as well as promoting and conducting research on learning, teaching, and assessment. Their five-year funding cycle from NSF has ended, but it is hoped that this will not be the end of the innovative work they have done.

---

[1]These textbooks are listed for illustrative purposes, and this list does not constitute an endorsement of their content by the National Research Council.

Interdisciplinary Textbooks: Some Examples

- Berg, H.C., 1993. *Random Walks in Biology.* Princeton University Press. Written to sharpen the intuition of biologists about the statistics of molecules. The book focuses on diffusion. Topics range from the one-dimensional random walk to the motile behavior of bacteria .
- Cavalli-Sforza, L.L., 2000. *Genes, Peoples, and Languages.* North Point Press. A view of the last hundred thousand years of human evolution based on combining information from three disciplines—genetics, archaeology, and linguistics.
- Denny, M.W., 1993. *Air and Water: The Biology and Physics of Life's Media.* Princeton University Press. Presentation of the basic principles of physics as they apply to air and water, followed by many interesting biological illustrations (e.g., Why are eggs so fragile?).
- Edelstein-Keshet, L., 1988. *Mathematical Models in Biology.* Birkhauser. Summary of modern mathematical methods currently used in modeling, and examples of applications of mathematics to real-life problems.
- Hoppensteadt, F.C. and Peskin, C.S., 1992. *Mathematics in Medicine and the Life Sciences.* Springer. Presentation of topics drawn mainly from population biology (e.g., demographics, population biology, epidemics) and physiology (e.g., blood flow, gas exchange, renal countercurrent mechanism, biological clocks and neural control) that have benefited from mathematical modeling and analysis.
- Howard, J., 2001. *Mechanics of Motor Proteins and the Cytoskeleton.* Sinauer. Presentation of physical principles (mechanical, thermal, and chemical forces) underlying biomolecular mechanics, followed by a detailed exposition of the structure, mechanics, and force-generation mechanisms of the cytoskeleton and motor proteins.
- Murray, J.D., 1993. *Mathematical Biology* (2nd ed.). Springer. Presentation of mathematical models that provide insight into biological processes. Topics include population biology, biological oscillators and switches, pattern formation, biological waves, and infectious disease dynamics.
- Taubes, C.H., 2001. *Modeling Differential Equations in Biology.* Prentice Hall. Based on a differential equation course at Harvard designed for life science students who have had only the basics of calculus. In each chapter, mathematical principles pertinent to a biological problem are developed and applied. Each chap-

---

Interdisciplinary Textbooks: Some Examples
Continued

ter also contains several biological research articles illustrating the power of differential equations and analysis in gaining a deeper understanding of biological questions. These papers deal with topics such as *Scope of the AIDS Epidemic in the United States*, *Experimentally Induced Transitions in the Dynamic Behavior of Insect Populations*, and *Thresholds in Development*.

• Vogel, S., 1998. *Cats' Paws and Catapults: Mechanical Worlds of Nature and People*. Norton. An introduction to biomechanics. Compares nature's solutions with those arising from human technology.

It should be noted here that preparation of such modules is no small task and will require a major commitment of time and effort. The collaborating faculty do not all need to teach at the same institution, especially if financial support is provided by foundations, agencies, or societies. Because of the huge commitment, it is efficient for two or more faculty to collaborate in development, and for the results to be widely disseminated. This is only possible if they receive adequate support from their own institution and other organizations that fund biology education. Issues related to the creation of additional teaching materials and the design of new approaches are further discussed in Chapter 6: Implementation.

4

Engaging Students with Interdisciplinary and Project-based Laboratories

RECOMMENDATION #4

Laboratory courses should be as interdisciplinary as possible, since laboratory experiments that confront students with real-world observations do not separate well into conventional disciplines.

THE ROLE OF LABORATORIES

Science courses and the laboratories associated with them should cultivate the ability of students to think independently. They should provide students with exposure to realistic scientific questions and highlight those aspects that are inherently interdisciplinary. They can also provide opportunities for students to learn to work cooperatively in groups. The committee recommends that project-based laboratories with discovery components replace traditional scripted "cookbook" laboratories to develop the capacity of students to tackle increasingly challenging projects with greater independence.

Laboratories can illustrate and build on the concepts covered in the classroom. Once students have time to examine the specimens, materials, and equipment described in class, they will be better prepared to carry out experiments. The purpose of restructuring the emphasis of the teaching laboratory is to stimulate student interest and participation. Project-based laboratories are also choice arenas for developing the scientific writing, speaking, and presentation skills of students.

Interdisciplinary laboratories are a promising means of strengthening the physical science and quantitative background of life science majors and of introducing biology to uncommitted students or those majoring in other fields. Harvey Mudd College has developed an introductory laboratory course consisting of three-week interdisciplinary experiments that are open-ended and highly investigative. The goal of the laboratory course, called ID Lab, is to help students understand the research approach in science and the natural relationship between biology and other scientific disciplines. Case Study #6 illustrates one way to strengthen undergraduate education by making learning a highly active experience from the first day of college.

The other case studies (#7 and #8) and examples presented here are project-based laboratories that can engage students and cultivate independent learning. This is not meant to be an exhaustive list, but rather an array of examples that illustrate what can be done, and what is now being done, at institutions nationwide.

PROPOSED NEW LABORATORIES

Not all schools will find it practical to adopt a completely project-based approach to their physics courses. If the traditional lecture is retained, modifications can still be made to the laboratory component of the course. Two ideas for getting started are included here. The first retains a straight physics approach, while the second incorporates ideas from engineering.

A Proposed Physics Laboratory Based on a "Crawl, Walk, Run" Approach

The physics laboratory can be used to introduce new concepts, in addition to its traditional use of reinforcing concepts already presented in lecture. Some concepts are best learned through laboratory exploration, such as error analysis, uncertainty, fluctuations, and noise. Furthermore, examples drawn from biology can be introduced in the section on Newtonian and macroscopic mechanics, as well as in other areas. Properties of materials (e.g., bone, tendon, hair), biological fluid flows, and motions of bacteria or bioparticles in water provide excellent opportunities. The laboratory is also a choice arena to teach principles of engineering as they apply to biology.

The "crawl, walk, run" approach is one means of developing the capacity of students to tackle increasingly challenging projects with greater independence. This three-step model can gradually teach students to think through a process and carry out experiments on their own in order to acquire a conceptual understanding of the topics. In the "crawl" phase, students are given step-by-step instruction and data sheets to record their observations. In the "walk" phase, they are given guidelines and examples of how experiments might be carried out, but not explicit directions. In the "run" phase, they are given open-ended questions to explore and answer. The duration of laboratory modules would range from one week in the crawl phase to three weeks or even longer in the run phase. Students benefit from the interactions required to perform laboratory work in teams of two or three students. However, it is often necessary to require that writing be done individually, in order to assess learning and to encourage the students to further develop their writing skills. By the run phase, students would be able to hand in a short report explaining the problem studied, the methods used, and their findings, and also give a brief oral report.

It may not be feasible to have a physical lab for all the desired laboratory experiences. Physical laboratories are generally preferred, but both physical and virtual labs can be utilized. LabVIEW (*http://sine.ni.com/apps/ we/nioc.vp?cid=1381&lang=US*) and Matlab (*http://www.mathworks.com/ products/matlab/*) both offer excellent environments for students to learn laboratory skills and concepts. These software packages use mathematical computing to facilitate data acquisition, data analysis, creation of algorithms, and data visualization. Web-based learning is most useful when particular experiments are not available or may be hard to reproduce locally.

Ideas for crawl- and walk-phase experiments related to conservation of energy and Newtonian mechanics are listed here; ideas for the run phase follow. The choice of topics for crawl or walk sessions would be determined by the instructor, taking into account the syllabus for any accompanying course, the students' backgrounds, and available equipment.

- *Conservations of energy:* energy input and storage, basal metabolism, measurement of energy expenditure, external and/or internal mechanical work, and energy efficiency.
- *Newtonian mechanics:* muscles as force actuators, moments created by muscles, free body diagram analysis within the context of human joint mechanics, ground reaction forces, mechanics of gait-running, and standing balance, calculation of the center of pressure and center of reaction,

CASE STUDY #6
Interdisciplinary Laboratory
Harvey Mudd College

In Harvey Mudd's Interdisciplinary Laboratory (ID Lab), all experiments include technique development, instrumental experience, question formation and hypothesis testing, data and error analysis, oral and written reporting, and, most importantly, the opportunity to explore in an open-ended way some of the details of phenomena that are familiar and of interest to students. In several experiments, the students visually study molecular interactions via molecular modeling software that is installed on the laptops they use in the laboratory. Finally, students are paired with a different partner for each module, developing teamwork skills in the process, and they share and discuss their experimental results after each module, gaining a sense for collective work in science.

A variety of assessment efforts have been used to evaluate the lab course, including student evaluations after individual modules and at the end of each semester. The student response to the course has been very positive, particularly in regard to the interdisciplinary nature of the experiments. At the end of the 1999-2000 course, an assessment exercise was administered to the ID Lab students and those enrolled in the regular chemistry lab sequence. The ID students were also completing the second semester of the regular chemistry lab course, and the other students were completing the first semester of the physics lab sequence. Thus, both groups had completed three semesters of lab coursework at that point. The result of the exercise, which was evaluated by a faculty member from another college, was that the ID students and the other students performed equally on many measures, but the ID students showed higher-level thinking skills for developing hypotheses, designing creative experiments to test those hypotheses, and identifying sources of experimental error (in-house assessment data).

A secondary outgrowth of the development and implementation of this laboratory has been faculty development. If students are to be encouraged in their interdisciplinary thinking, faculty must also think along these same interdisciplinary lines, an approach to teaching and learning that is not always natural or comfortable for college faculty. The ID Lab has promoted cross-disciplinary understanding by the faculty and, as such, is a positive step toward encouraging students to think about disciplinary connections.

Finally, the lab requires that students apply rigorous quantitative approaches to analyzing their experimental work, thus helping them see the importance of studying further mathematics and computer science if they are going to solve important problems in the life sciences. While it is too early to tell whether the lab will lead students in mathematics, computer science, or the physical sciences to pursue careers in the life sciences, or whether those who were planning on studying biology will take a more quantitative path toward their career, it seems possible that such results may occur.

Some of the laboratory exercises that ID Lab students conduct include:

- Thermal properties of an ectothermic animal: Are lizards just cylinders with legs?
- Molecular weight of macromolecules: Is molecular weight always simple?
- Mechanical resonance of a high-rise building: Are seismic nightmares avoidable?
- Carbonate content of biological hard tissue: Of what are shells composed?
- Using digital logic to time a simple pendulum: What makes a good clock?
- A structure-activity investigation of photosynthetic electron transport: How does a biological system convert physics into chemistry?
- Synthesis and characterization of liquid crystals: Or when are liquids not?
- A genetic map of a bacterial plasmid: Where are the restriction sites?

For more information: *http://www2.hmc.edu/~karukstis/IDLab/1999_2000/home.htm*

CASE STUDY #7
Neurobiology Laboratory
Harvard University

An inquiry-based approach to neuroscience at Harvard University uses state-of-the-art technology to study the development and function of the nervous system. Each of four faculty members leads a three-week laboratory module centered on a common theme. This one-semester course meets for three hours, twice weekly. Because the experiments are open-ended, students can spend additional time in the laboratory as desired. For each module, students prepare a report describing their experimental results and interpretation.

In the following example, the course was centered on the visual system. The themes of the four modules were:

(1) *Visual processing in the retina*. Students examined electrical recording of action potentials from retinal ganglion cells of the salamander. They analyzed the neural code for visual signals, in particular temporal integration and color processing. Methods used included dissection, extracellular recording, pharmacology, and spike train analysis.

(2) *Cellular electrophysiology*. Students performed patch clamp analysis of horizontal cells isolated from the retina. They studied the various electrical conductances of the neuronal membrane, including how they are activated by changes in voltage and binding of ligands. Methods used included current clamp and voltage clamp recording, light microscopy, and pharmacological studies.

(3) *Development of the visual system in Drosophila*. Topics included how molecules direct axon guidance, the mechanisms that determine neural connectivity throughout development. Methods used included microdissection, immunohistochemistry, video microscopy, confocal microscopy, and mutant analysis.

(4) *Circadian rhythms in the suprachiasmatic nucleus*. Students observed neural firing in the brain's biological clock, how it varies rhythmically with time of day, and how it is entrained by the environmental light cycle. They monitored corresponding changes in gene transcription for molecular components of the clock. Methods used included brain slice dissection, extracellular recording, and PCR amplification.

For more information: *http://www.mcb.harvard.edu/Education/Undergrad/Biochem/int_and_adv_courses.html*

inverse dynamics modeling of a simplified foot to determine ankle reaction forces, moments, and powers; and force control within the context of motor control.

Laboratory exercises on the above topics could also include a special emphasis on the numerical and mathematical analysis of experiments. For example, students studying the inverse dynamics model of a mass and spring could use an experimental setup including an accelerometer on the mass, and a spring supported by a load cell. Students would measure the mass location using an encoder or potentiometer. They would take measurements while the system oscillates and use inverse dynamics to calculate the spring force. The calculation can be done using two different methods. One method of calculation would require them to numerically low-pass filter the location data and then numerically differentiate the location data to achieve acceleration as a function of time and calculate the spring force. In the second method, they would calculate the spring force using the acceleration data and an idealized mathematical model of the mass, spring stiffness, and initial conditions. The group could then discuss the similarities and differences between the two descriptions of the spring force.

In the run phase, the labs would each last approximately three weeks, to give students an opportunity to consider each area in depth. Topics could include sensors, data acquisition systems, signal processing, or computational analysis of data. The labs would be designed to give students the ability to characterize, specify, analyze, and integrate devices. Labs could be centered on applications relevant to modern biological research or clinical biomedical studies such as these examples:

- *The human eye:* optical measurements, structure of the eye, functioning of the eye, the optical system of the eye, the response system of the eye, resolution of the eye, the eye's response to varying illumination, depth perception, or defects of vision.
- *Biomedical measurement:* cell, nerve, and muscle potentials; electrocardiograms (ECG), electromyograms (EMG), body temperature, control of body temperature, heat loss from the body, blood pressure measurement, blood flow and volume measurements, noninvasive blood-gas sensors, optical microscopy, cell adhesion, optical sources and sensors, lung volume, heart sounds, drug delivery devices, surgical instruments, or electroshock protection.
- *Medical imaging:* origin of x-rays, the x-ray beam, attenuation and

**CASE STUDY #8
Workshop Physics
Dickinson College**

Project-based teaching has completely replaced traditional lecture and laboratory teaching in a physics course entitled Workshop Physics, pioneered at Dickinson College in 1986. Workshop Physics uses guided inquiry workshops featuring computers and specially designed equipment to help students learn by doing. Inquiry-based cooperative learning is combined with the comprehensive use of computer tools for data acquisition, data analysis, and mathematical modeling. Students meet in three two-hour sessions each week. There are no formal lectures. Each section has one instructor, two undergraduate teaching assistants, and up to 24 students. Each pair of students shares the use of a microcomputer and an extensive collection of scientific apparatus and other gadgets. Among other things, students pitch baseballs, whack bowling balls with rubber hammers, pull objects up inclined planes, attempt pirouettes, build electronic circuits, explore electrical unknowns, ignite paper with compressed gas, and devise engine cycles using rubber bands. The Workshop labs are staffed during evening and weekend hours with undergraduate teaching assistants.

Kinematics, Newton's laws of motion, conservation laws, rotational motion, and oscillations are studied in the first semester. The second semester covers thermodynamics, electricity, electronics, and magnetism. The material is divided into units lasting about one week. Students use an activity guide (e.g., Laws, *Workshop Physics Activity Guide,* 1997), which has expositions, questions, and instructions as well as blank spaces for student data, calculations, and reflections. The guide is keyed to a standard textbook.

Microcomputer-based laboratory tools (called MBL tools) are used extensively to collect, analyze, and display data. An MBL station consists of a sensor or probe that is plugged into a microcom-

absorption of x-rays, x-ray filters, beam size, radiographic image, production of x-rays, computed tomography, ultrasound, MRI, nuclear imaging, single-photon emission computed tomography, or positron emission tomography.

puter via an electronic interface (e.g., *www.vernier.com* and *www.pasco.com*). Sensors that have been linked directly to the computer include an ultrasonic motion detector, photogates, temperature sensors, light probes, pressure sensors, currents and voltage probes, magnetic field sensors, rotary motion sensors, and Geiger tubes. With a new generation of MBL software developed at Tufts University, the computer can perform instantaneous calculations and produce real-time graphs. Software features allow users to enter new calculations into the software for the real-time display of derived quantities. For example, position vs. time data acquired using the motion sensor can be used to calculate kinetic energy vs. time data in real time. The software also allows users to perform FFT analysis, do curve fitting and modeling, and find derivatives and integrals for selected portions of the data. Data can also be transferred easily to a spreadsheet for additional analysis. Video analysis tools allow students to capture and digitize two-dimensional motion.

About two-thirds of the students who have taken Workshop Physics strongly prefer this method to the lecture approach. Although the conceptual gains of Workshop Physics students are greater than those achieved by students taking conventional physics courses in many topic areas, the gains are not universal, and in certain areas Workshop Physics students perform no better than their traditional peers. Student performance in upper-level physics courses and in solving traditional textbook problems is as good as or better than that of students in the traditional curriculum. Moreover, Workshop Physics students demonstrate a comparatively greater degree of comfort working with computers and other laboratory equipment.

For more information: *http://physics.dickinson.edu/ Workshop_Physics/Workshop_Physics_Home.htm*

A Proposed Engineering-for-Life-Scientists Laboratory

One way to engage students with engineering concepts important to biology is through an "engineering-for-life-scientist" laboratory. This idea is presented here because it was suggested as an alternative to a physics lab by the panel on physics and engineering. It could also be adapted for teaching as an independent course or as the laboratory component of a biology course. The laboratory described here follows a similar crawl, walk, run format as the physics laboratory proposed above. Students would obtain hands-on experiences with how the basic laws of physics control life from an engineering perspective. This approach would also be synergistic with the idea of integrating more engineering concepts into biology courses. Students would consider the following types of questions: What solutions did nature find to solving a certain problem? How does the system function? What are the crucial functional elements? Why do they work together? These are essentially engineering questions.

The crawl phase would focus on the ramifications of Newton's mechanics:

• Conservation of energy: energy input and storage, measurement of energy consumption, external and/or internal mechanical work, energy efficiency.
• Muscles as force actuators; moments created by muscles; calculating the point of gravity; force analysis of a system with one, two, and more joints; set-up a mass-spring system. Attach an accelerometer to the mass, and measure the response.
• Building a simple robotic system that can move and carrying out a mechanical analysis of the construct.

The walk phase would focus on electrical phenomena ranging from charges and charge separation in solution, to electronics and instrumentation:

• Building RC circuits; mimicking an action potential of a nerve cell; simple coupled RC circuits. Circuit analysis.
• Osmotic pressure versus hydrostatic pressure; building a cell; pressure measurements; analysis of systems with varying pore sizes and/or sizes of charged particles. Modeling the kinetics of charge separation.
• Visualizing and analyzing the path of charged molecules/particles in microfluidic devices. Experimentation and modeling.

The run phase would focus on optics and spectroscopy. Optical microscopy has emerged as a primary experimental tool for biologists, so students would learn the basic optical laws, as well as the essential components and methods in optical microscopy. Fluorophores are frequently employed by biologists as spectroscopic probes. The way that fluorophores absorb and emit light and the competing de-excitation pathways by which fluorophores can give off their energy are important concepts. Proper analysis of the signals and images captured with optical microscopes is crucial to avoid misinterpretation of data and erroneous conclusions. Assuming that in the future optics will play a stronger role in the classroom physics curriculum, the following topics could be covered:

- Building a human eye from optical components. Analysis of its performance; corrective optics for the human eye.
- Light sources and optical components (filters, lenses, lambda/half and lambda/quarter plates, polarizers).
- Introduction to optical microscopy; illumination, building of a simple telescope or microscope.
- Differential interference microscopy.
- Confocal microscopy.
- Photophysics of light absorption and emission, competing deactivation pathways; kinetic analysis.

Chemistry Laboratory

Chemistry laboratory courses frequently focus on teaching specific research techniques. Experience indicates that students are more excited about courses in which they feel they are discovering something new, not just trying to duplicate an established experiment. The two objectives can be combined into a project-based laboratory. For example, in a synthetic organic chemistry experiment, different groups of students could perform the reaction at different temperatures. This would enable them to determine a rate constant for the reaction, and also its energy of activation, and for different times, to see the effect on yield of the product. Another possibility is to determine the effect of reaction conditions, such as the duration of synthesis, on the ratio of the desired product to other products. All of this is relevant to optimizing a synthesis, a common real-life research goal in industry. The variation in results among students performing the same experiment would also introduce them to statistical analysis of experimental data.

Chemistry laboratory courses are also excellent places to teach some fundamental aspects of the science. For example, infrared and nuclear magnetic resonance spectroscopies are most appreciated if students examine "unknowns" by these techniques and then deduce their chemical structures, perhaps also being given a mass spectrum.

Some simple experiments with enzymes can teach a lot. For example, students as a class can follow an enzymatic reaction using optical spectroscopy of quenched samples (so they do not need to tie up the spectrometers) at different times, but with varying pH's and/or the addition of inhibitors with varying substrate concentrations. This would let them determine and try to understand the rate laws involved and the reason for a pH dependence.

Genomics Laboratory

Project-based laboratories are also well suited for the acquisition of computer and programming skills. Genomics lends itself particularly well to project-based learning. For example, students could be asked to carry out computer searches to track down what is known about a particular gene. This would involve exploring (1) the internal structure of the gene: exons, introns, promoter, and transcription factor binding sites; (2) how its expression is regulated; (3) homologs, orthologs, and other aspects of its evolution; (4) the structure and function of the protein; (5) interactions of the protein with other proteins and with small molecules; and (6) diseases caused by mutations in the coding and noncoding regions of the gene. Students in such a laboratory could also be presented with challenges such as predicting alternative splicing patterns or three-dimensional structure.

Sophisticated project-based experiments in genomics are being carried out by undergraduates at many institutions using DNA arrays. The Genome Consortium for Active Teaching (GCAT), founded at Davidson College and now comprising more than 35 faculty members around the country, has made DNA arrays accessible to undergraduates for original experiments in which the expression levels of many genes are monitored for pairs of distinctive biological states (e.g., growth in a rich versus a minimal medium). The consortium provides yeast, *Arabidopsis,* and *E. coli* expression arrays at a relatively modest price. Protocols for the preparation of RNA and for hybridization are also provided. Undergraduates carry out the biological experiments, isolate the mRNA, and perform the hybridization. The arrays are then sent to GCAT for scanning on their array reader. Students analyze the resulting expression data to determine which genes are differentially expressed and to pose questions for further experimentation.

5

Enabling Undergraduates to Experience the Excitement of Biology

INCORPORATING INDEPENDENT UNDERGRADUATE RESEARCH EXPERIENCES

RECOMMENDATION #5

All students should be encouraged to pursue independent research as early as is practical in their education. They should be able to receive academic credit for independent research done in collaboration with faculty or with off-campus researchers.

> *"Undergraduate research is not only the essential component of good teaching and effective learning, but also that research with undergraduate students is in itself the purest form of teaching."*
>
> Quote from committee member James M. Gentile in *Academic Excellence,* a report of the Research Corporation on the role of research at undergraduate institutions (Research Corporation and Doyle, 2000)

Many research scientists regard their undergraduate research experience as a turning point that led them to pursue research careers (Doyle, 2000; Hakim, 2000; Rothman and Narum, 1999). By working as a partner in an active research group, undergraduates experience the rewards and frustrations of original research. They learn from mentors, who can be faculty, industrial scientists, postdoctoral fellows, and sometimes graduate students (NRC, 1997b). They can gain experience working as part of a team and learn effective oral and written presentation of scientific results. A written thesis as a product of the undergraduate research experience can be an opportunity for a student to learn to review a field and coherently describe his or her contribution. Such undergraduate research sometimes leads to peer-reviewed publications and student presentations at national and international scientific meetings. While the richness of experience for the student likely will not be the same as working in a research group, it also is possible to provide meaningful research experiences for undergraduates in research-based courses or in teaching laboratories that are designed to be open-ended and to encourage independent investigation.

At smaller schools, undergraduates often work directly with a faculty member or in a research group consisting of a faculty member and other undergraduates. At larger institutions, such as research universities, undergraduates become part of a research group along with graduate students and postdoctoral fellows. Early career faculty who have not yet built up large research groups can play a particularly effective role in providing research opportunities for undergraduates. Sometimes participation in research can even begin in formal laboratory courses, in which students become involved in the research of the teaching fellows, other students, or the faculty. While undergraduates can derive much education and inspiration from these advanced students, it is important that they still have significant interaction with their faculty mentors. Undergraduates should in all cases play a full role, giving oral reports to the group on their research and participating in all group seminars and social events.

It is important for institutions to realize that the time faculty spend mentoring undergraduates in the laboratory is teaching and should be recognized as such. This is a particularly important issue for pretenure faculty. The faculty investment in mentoring and guiding student research represents a large commitment of time and resources. This must be recognized as an important teaching responsibility and integrated into the overall workload of the faculty member. At the same time, students should receive appropriate course credit for their research. The National Research Council's *Adviser, Teacher, Role Model, Friend: On Being a Mentor to Students in Science and Engineering* (NRC, 1997a) can assist faculty in this important role.

Undergraduate research is a discovery-driven effort that must be carried out in the setting of a strong and supportive natural science community. A key factor in the program is the close professional partnership between the student and faculty member. While faculty members may be excellent research scholars, they are not necessarily all equally adept at being research mentors for undergraduate students. Indeed, many institutions make attempts to train good mentors by holding workshops for faculty and graduate and postdoctoral students, and by pairing junior faculty with successful and respected senior faculty as peer mentors. In the best of circumstances, the faculty mentor works in the laboratory with the student, resulting in extensive informal student-faculty interaction and helping the student to build self-confidence in the research endeavor. The mentor guides the student in all aspects of the scientific process, including literature searches, experimental design, construction and/or operation of scientific equipment, carrying out experiments, and interpreting results. The mentor also assists the student in professional development, including giving course advice, discussing career path options, and introducing students to key individuals at graduate institutions. Faculty play the lead role in educating students to effectively communicate their research results through regular group meetings, weekly student research seminars in the summer, presentations at off-campus research symposia, poster preparation, and manuscript writing. Student attendance at regional and national meetings with their mentors should be a priority. When individual mentoring is combined with excellent science, the student becomes strengthened not only in a particular research agenda, but also gains a foundation for success in science that extends beyond the immediate institution.

Many undergraduates get their sole experience doing independent laboratory research in the summer. In biology, most of those students go to universities where they are supported by the Research Experiences for Undergraduates (REU) Program of the National Science Foundation or undergraduate education grants from the Howard Hughes Medical Institute. These programs are predicated on the notion that an active research experience is one of the most effective ways to attract talented undergraduates to science and to retain them in science and engineering careers. These programs stress the importance of interactions between students and faculty or other research mentors in addition to research productivity at larger institutions. For smaller schools with insufficient campus research opportunities, summer research both for students and faculty is vital to the educational development and enrichment of life sciences majors. However, research takes time and where possible, the continuation of summer research throughout the year, even if a few hours a week, can greatly increase the learning experience.

Other groups are also active in promoting research experiences. The Council on Undergraduate Research (CUR) is a network of faculty members devoted to providing experiences for undergraduates. CUR has 3,000 members representing over 850 institutions in eight academic divisions. Most members are from primarily undergraduate institutions. CUR encourages faculty-student collaborative research and investigative teaching strategies, as well as supports faculty development and attempts to attract attention to the benefits of undergraduate research. Additional information is available at *http://www.cur.org*. Professional societies, such as the American Society for Microbiology (ASM), also play an active role in stimulating undergraduate education and research. ASM often holds sessions on education at its annual meetings and provides independent conferences on education such as the Ninth ASM Undergraduate Microbiology Education Conference entitled "Emerging Issues in Microbiology: Expanding Education Horizons." Additional information is available at *http://www. asmusa.org/*. An extensive annotated list of professional societies active in undergraduate science education, as well as links to other resources for science education, can be found at the Sigma Xi Web site: *http:// www.sigmaxi.org/resources/overview/index.shtml.*

Opportunities for learning also exist beyond the classroom and the faculty laboratory. The range of research opportunities available to undergraduates can be further broadened by drawing on the strengths of a wide range of public and private institutions. Independent work in faculty laboratories, biotechnology companies, pharmaceutical companies, agricultural chemistry companies, engineering firms, national labs, and independent research centers should be encouraged. Real-world research is generally more interdisciplinary than traditional lab courses. Biotechnology companies, as well as established pharmaceutical and agricultural chemistry companies, have a major stake in the vitality and quality of undergraduate education for future research biologists. Industry will employ many life sciences majors in the years ahead. To abet the academic advising process, they and their teachers need to acquire an understanding of the spectrum of industry activities from basic research through product development. The formation of partnerships between life science corporations and academic institutions can enhance student learning in the undergraduate years so that scientists of the future prepare to play leadership roles in the private sector. Such partnerships could consist of summer or academic year research internships for students.

Another possible collaboration would be corporate sponsorship of undergraduate research on college or university campuses. Corporate sponsorship for faculty to work in industry during summers or sabbaticals would help transfer knowledge into the academic setting. Similar types of benefits might be possible by arranging for scientists and engineers employed by local companies to regularly come to campus and interact with faculty and students.

Many independent research institutes also offer summer programs that provide students with opportunities for laboratory work at very high levels using the most modern equipment. For example, Cold Spring Harbor has carried out for many years an Undergraduate Research Program that has been very successful in encouraging students to enter the profession, and has given others an appreciation of how research is done. Colleges and universities should make maximum use of such research opportunities, and both public and private research institutes should be encouraged to develop undergraduate research programs.

Biology undergraduates also should be given opportunities to study and carry out research in foreign countries to broaden their education and enhance their appreciation of the international nature of science Case Study #9). As research science is increasingly an international endeavor, future researchers will benefit from experiences that give them the opportunity to work with researchers from other countries in Web partnerships or other projects, or to spend time in research laboratories in other countries. The University of California at Irvine maintains a list of programs available for undergraduates to do research abroad at *http://www.cie.uci.edu/iop/research.html*

SEMINARS TO COMMUNICATE
THE EXCITEMENT OF BIOLOGY

RECOMMENDATION #6

Seminar-type courses that highlight cutting-edge developments in biology should be provided on a continual and regular basis throughout the four-year undergraduate education of students. Communicating the excitement of biological research is crucial to attracting, retaining, and sustaining a greater diversity of students to the field. These courses would combine presentations by faculty with student projects on research topics.

Real problems reveal the connections between the different scientific disciplines. One benefit of using real examples is the demonstration to

---

CASE STUDY #9
Undergraduate Research Abroad
University of Arizona

BRAVO! (Biomedical Research Abroad: Vistas Open) gives re-search-experienced undergraduate students an opportunity to become part of the international scientific community by conducting research in another country. With funding from the Howard Hughes Medical Institute, Minority International Research Training (MIRT) Grants from the NIH Fogarty International Center, and NSF's Recognition Award for the Integration of Research & Education Program (RAIRE), the BRAVO! program has sent 88 undergraduate students, 9 graduate students, and 6 minority faculty members from the University of Arizona (UA) to work in 23 countries since 1992. In addition, 15 foreign faculty mentors and 16 foreign graduate students have made research visits to UA. BRAVO! aims to help students learn to do research in a different cultural setting while gaining independence and confidence. It tries to inspire them to discover who they are as Americans, by providing an opportunity to contribute to the worldwide scientific community.

In the early years of the program students generally spent only a summer doing research abroad. More recently, the trend has been toward longer foreign stays since these result in more scientifically productive visits. The level of productivity is shown by the 61 publications and more than 65 presentations at scientific meetings that include the work of BRAVO! students. In addition to benefiting indi-

---

students with a quantitative bent that biology is not a purely descriptive science. These courses should be offered to all students; however, they are especially important for first-year students in colleges where biology courses are normally started only in the sophomore year. Through such courses, biology students can retain and increase their interest in the field.

Recent advances in biological research are exciting; exposing students to the current research at an early stage in their education will help them to see this excitement. Research can be presented by inviting faculty or other scientists to talk about their work; it does not necessarily require students to work in labs immediately. Presenting students with numerous questions that remain to be answered encourages them to imagine their own future role in research. Topics and faculty members should be chosen carefully, vidual students and science in general, BRAVO! gives the undergraduate curriculum at UA a more international perspective. Upon returning from abroad, each BRAVO! student gives a "datablitz" (presentation of research and experience accompanied by a meal typical of food in the country visited) to students, faculty, family, and friends. Students also write an article for the monthly Undergraduate Biology Research Program newsletter.

BRAVO! helps prepare students for the international nature of today's world. It recognizes that the problems facing humankind cut across national boundaries. For example, an increase in vector insect populations in northern Mexico has implications for the spread of diseases such as dengue fever into the United States. Modern travel leads to the spread of infectious diseases, such as West Nile fever, previously known only in developing countries, and spreads diseases such as TB, HIV, and AIDS throughout the world. To understand and treat such diseases requires not only scientific knowledge, but also the ability and the will to work with people from other cultures. BRAVO! provides an innovative model for how research universities can internationalize the curriculum for science students. Similar programs at other institutions have developed as others recognize that undergraduates can thrive in an international research setting.

For more information: *http://www.blc.arizona.edu/UBRP/bravo/ default.html*

with an eye to the type of material and presentations that will engage students with limited scientific backgrounds. As a supplement, students could investigate a topic related to one of the presentations. Their investigations could include finding review articles or interviewing graduate students or post-docs in the faculty member's lab. More ideas along these lines are presented in the report *Transforming Undergraduate Education in Science, Mathematics, Engineering and Technology* (NRC, 1999b, p. 5). One program that advocates the idea of engaging students by presenting science in context is called SENCER (Science Education for New Civic Engagements and Responsibilities) and is organized by the American Association of Colleges and Universities. SENCER attempts "to connect science and civic engagement by teaching, through complex and unsolved public issues, such as natural catastrophes, water quality, HIV disease, the Human Genome Project, energy alternatives, and nuclear disarmament," according to its Web site (*http://www.aacu-edu.org/sencer/*).

Many students enter college more interested in interdisciplinary courses or seminars than in the traditional introductory science courses. Others have not decided on their major when they enroll. Interdisciplinary courses are a useful way to provide students with exposure to science without limiting their potential choice of majors. Interdisciplinary courses are also prime spots to convey the spirit of science and examples of unsolved problems that are ripe for attack. They are appropriate for students of all levels, but can be used specifically for first-year students to excite their interest.

Physics, chemistry, and mathematics underlie much of biology and it is therefore advantageous for students to take courses in those fields early in a scientific career. This means that some potential biology majors do not take a biology course until their sophomore year. The appropriate inclusion of biological topics in chemistry, mathematics, and physics somewhat alleviates this difficulty, but they are not a totally adequate substitute for a true biology course. One way to address that problem is to design an interdisciplinary course linking the various scientific disciplines. For example the Science One program at the University of British Columbia is designed for first-year students as an integrated sequence that melds the topics together, giving students a sense of interconnections right from the start of their collegiate career (Case Study #10). For students taking more traditional science courses, a seminar of this type described can be appealing. Another seminar designed for first-year students is described in Case Study #11. This course could be modified for more advanced students, or another seminar centered around an exciting biological theme like infectious diseases could be designed.

INCREASING THE DIVERSITY OF
FUTURE RESEARCH BIOLOGISTS

To increase the number of qualified students considering a career in biological research, the committee discussed diversifying the applicant pool through two ways: increasing the number of students who are majoring in other sciences and making the life sciences more accessible to students of both sexes and from all populations.

CASE STUDY #10
Integrated First-Year Science
University of British Columbia

Science One is a first-year integrated science sequence that presents biology, chemistry, math, and physics in a unified format. This 25-credit course includes lectures, laboratories, and tutorials. Students who complete Science One satisfy requirements for entry into all second-year courses in UBC's Faculty of Science. The program emphasizes critical, independent thought as the basis of scientific inquiry. Students are encouraged to ask focused questions, suggest solutions, communicate, discuss, and defend their findings, ideas, and visions.

Scientific coursework covers topics from multiple different angles. For example, waves are presented as physical and mathematical descriptions of classical phenomena and then related to the quantum nature of matter. Each year a field trip to a marine research station provides field and laboratory exposure to shoreline ecology, marine biology, physical oceanography, and chemical ecology.

Lou Gass, a Science One faculty member, has also created "Science First," a series of informal lunchtime seminars in which faculty talk about their research, why they became scientists, and what science means to them. He says, "Students come boiling out of Science One and are causing a ruckus in their other classes because they hear something and their hand goes up. Once students get their curiosity tweaked and start making connections they take off like a rocket" (University of British Columbia, 1996).

For more information: *http://www.science.ubc.ca/~science1/*

Making Biology Attractive and Accessible to
Majors in Other Sciences

Undergraduates majoring in the physical sciences, mathematics, and computer science will constitute an even larger proportion of the research community in the life sciences in the years ahead because of the heightened importance of these disciplines for biological research and the reach of many aspects of the life sciences into these other disciplines. The committee recommends that these students be given a sense of the excitement of biology

CASE STUDY #11
First-Year Seminar on Plagues
University of Oregon

This first-year seminar, Plagues: The Past, Present, and Future of Infectious Diseases, at the University of Oregon examines diseases such as malaria, bubonic plague, smallpox, polio, measles, and AIDS. In addition to the biology of the diseases, it also addresses their effects on populations and their influence on the course of history. Students investigate the conditions that influence the rate of spread of contagious diseases, and ways to prevent it. They discuss a number of ethical issues that arise in treating the sick, as well as development of policies intended to halt epidemics. Infectious diseases are used to introduce important ideas and issues from the life sciences and a variety of other disciplines. Approaches include reading assignments, film presentations, discussions, writing, and small group activities and projects.

One segment of the course uses readings, discussions, computer modeling and lab activities to help students understand (1) how the immune system works and why in some cases it doesn't; (2) why antibiotics work with some organisms but not others, and why many organisms are becoming resistant to antibiotics; (3) why so many new diseases seem to be suddenly appearing; (4) how vaccines work and why in some cases they don't; (5) how infectious diseases are transmitted; (6) why and how disease-causing organisms make humans sick; and (7) why most infectious diseases are usually not lethal.

Another segment examines the issue from a global perspective. Students study current global trends for diseases such as AIDS, malaria, and tuberculosis. They research the public health policies of international organizations and of representative countries; try to place these patterns into historical perspective; and develop some predictive models of the social, political, economic, and demographic consequences of these patterns.

A third segment examines what is happening locally. With the help of guest speakers, field trips, and group projects, they examine public health policies and practices in the state of Oregon, the city of Eugene, and at the University of Oregon. For example, they learn about vaccination and other public health programs offered at the Student Health Center and about the treatment of AIDS patients in Lane County.

For more information: *http://biology.uoregon.edu/Biology_www/Online_classes/Bi199w97u/syllabus.html*

and an appreciation of how the physical and mathematical sciences contribute to biological research.

Many outstanding research biologists were originally educated and trained in fields other than biology. Many geneticists and neurobiologists, for example, were educated as physicists. It is important for biologists to encourage the continued movement of other scientists and engineers into biological research. To this end, biologists need to convey the excitement of their field to students in other areas. The interdisciplinary or applied seminars mentioned in the previous section provide a good opportunity for interesting a wide variety of students, as they present material in a real-world context and can often illustrate topics that are relevant to students lives. It could also be advantageous for the future of research if some biologically trained students migrate toward specialties related to physical, information, and mathematical sciences. Their biological backgrounds will make them more approachable collaborators.

Students interested in highly quantitative approaches to biological research should be given opportunities throughout their undergraduate careers to develop their expertise in this domain. The committee recommends that schools establish and support interdepartmental programs that will enable these students to pursue quantitatively intense life science programs, such as biophysics, biomathematics, and computational biology.

Life science majors with an interest in and aptitude for mathematics and computer science should be encouraged to prepare for research and innovation at the interfaces of these disciplines and biology. These quantitatively oriented students will need a more extensive and deeper education in mathematics and computer science than is provided by the four-semester mathematics sequence mentioned earlier. Quantitatively oriented students should be permitted to take advanced mathematics and computer science courses in place of biology courses in meeting degree requirements. Biophysics major programs typically provide this flexibility, and new computational biology programs are also likely to do so (Case Study #12). A complementary approach is to establish interdisciplinary options or concentrations within existing majors. For example, biology courses normally taught with little quantitation could be expanded, using special sections, to teach relevant mathematical concepts. This could readily be accomplished in areas such as physiology, ecology, and genetics. Project-based courses with significant quantitative content would also be very appropriate. In addition, quantitatively oriented students can be given opportunities to develop software tools and programming skills in relation to biologically

CASE STUDY #12
Computational Biology
Carnegie Mellon University

Carnegie Mellon offers instruction in computational biology through three courses that are taught in a coordinated fashion. Students without programming experience who are interested in learning about the diverse ways in which computers are being used to solve biological problems can take Introduction to Computational Biology. This course has three major sections: Computational Molecular Biology (seven weeks, primarily focusing on sequence analysis), Biological Modeling (six weeks), and Biological Imaging (two weeks). Students with similar backgrounds but who are mainly interested in sequence analysis can take just the first half of the course. These courses are mainly taken by biology majors looking for basic knowledge of this important new field, as well as first-year biology PhD students who are *not* interested in doing their thesis in computational biology.

For students with strong programming skills and knowledge of computer science fundamentals, the computational biology course covers the same three topics in more detail. It makes use of the same lectures but has an additional one-hour class session per week in which methods are discussed with greater computational and mathematical sophistication, both through lectures and by reading papers from the literature. This course is taken by all computational biology majors, by double majors, by computer science majors with at least an introductory-level biology course, by biomedical engineering majors, and by computational chemistry students. It is also taken by first-year PhD students in biological sciences (interested in computational biology thesis projects), a few PhD students in computer science, and by computational biology MS students. The three courses combined typically have 40 students.

There are two major hallmarks to Carnegie Mellon's computational biology degree programs. Students receive extensive formal training in computer science by taking at least four courses from the normal undergraduate sequence in the School of Computer Science. This permits those students to be taught by faculty who are experts in computer science and gives them the skill set and vocabulary to frame computational problems and communicate with (non-biology-oriented) computer scientists. The second hallmark is the exposure of the students to a full range of computational biology topics, not just sequence-oriented methods.

For more information: *http://info.bio.cmu.edu/Programs/Undergraduate/compbio.html*

significant objectives. This could be accomplished by offering courses in database management systems, information systems, computer graphics, and computer simulation techniques.

At some schools, it will be optimal to offer majors in biophysics or computational biology; at others, select classes in those topics could be designed. Biochemistry is already a common major at many institutions, providing opportunities for students to explore the connections between those two fields.

Computational biology is not currently a common undergraduate major. Other schools that offer it include University of California at Santa Cruz; University of California at San Diego; Cornell University; University of Pennsylvania; Rensselaer Polytechnic University; Clark University; Towson University (Maryland); and Yale University.

Another undergraduate major that requires extensive use of quantitative skills is biophysics. The typical biophysics major takes three or four semesters each of mathematics and physics. The mathematics courses tend to cover the traditional subjects: calculus of one and more variables, linear algebra, and differential equations. In addition, students are generally required to take two upper-level biophysics courses. Some universities also have a physical chemistry requirement. Biophysics curricula should also have a broad biology component. The Biophysical Society provides a comprehensive listing of undergraduate biophysics programs at *http://www.biophysics.org/products/programs.htm*

Increasing the Ethnic, Cultural, and Gender Diversity of Life Science Majors

The retention and graduation of African American, Hispanic, and Native American students continues to be low. An NSF-sponsored project has shown that the most frequently cited reason for students of all backgrounds leaving science was the poor quality of the teaching they encountered in their science courses. They also state that poor K-12 preparation, difficulties with university courses, and the attraction of nonscientific disciplines diminish the number of minority students preparing for scientific careers (Seymour and Hewitt, 1997). A particularly serious problem is that such minority students often enter college with little exposure to the culture of science and find it difficult to see the relevance of their science courses to their future careers. The scientific establishment needs to find effective ways to gain access to this pool of potential scientific talent. Improving the quality of teaching in the sciences may help retain more students. The committee encourages programs designed to increase the diversity of life science majors.

While the curricular changes recommended in this report would improve the learning and skills of all students, it is important to consider that additional changes may be necessary to enable underrepresented minorities to fully achieve their potential as biomedical researchers. Summer bridge programs prior to entry into university, mentoring, study circles, and participation in integrated teams are often found to be helpful. Such initiatives should be made available to all students as needed, but focus should be on making biological education accessible to ethnic and cultural minorities who may have had less exposure to the sciences in their secondary education.

The NSF's Research Experiences for Undergraduates (REU) opportunities are an excellent way to reach broadly into the nation's student talent pool. The program provides students with the opportunity to be a part of a research lab and see for themselves what graduate education is like. NSF is particularly interested in increasing the participation in research of women, underrepresented minorities, and persons with disabilities. REU projects are strongly encouraged to involve students who are members of these groups. The success of these types of programs is critically dependent on the advising process. Students typically do not learn about such opportunities by themselves. They need ongoing faculty guidance and encouragement to steer them toward such programs.

Demonstrating that biological research is an exciting and appealing area of work is the best way to recruit and retain the most talented students. Interdisciplinary topics that reflect real examples of how science helps to alter and understand the world help convey that excitement. Interdisciplinary topics are also among the most studied today and undergraduate students who begin to grasp the connections between the various approaches to science will be well positioned to contribute to future research.

6

Implementation

Implementing the recommendations of this report will require a significant commitment of resources, both intellectual and financial. One important step is to consider the qualifications desired in a graduating biology major. For a school that is starting with a conventional modern biology curriculum, the committee envisions that multiple levels of transition would be necessary to fully incorporate physics, chemistry, mathematics, and engineering into the education of future biomedical researchers. Indeed a complete curriculum transformation would require alterations in departmental structures that may not be feasible in the short term. However, all institutions are capable of undertaking an initial stage of reform such as investigating how their teaching can better promote transfer of information among disciplines and the development and use of effective curricular modules in biology, physics, chemistry, mathematics, computer science, and engineering courses.

Creation of new interdisciplinary majors is a significant challenge, often necessitating the hiring of new faculty with experience doing interdisciplinary research and teaching interdisciplinary topics. Thus, a second stage in reform might target the development of new interdisciplinary courses for the math and physics curricula proposed here, together with new interdisciplinary laboratory courses. Subsequent steps might include the design of new interdisciplinary majors, searching for new faculty hires with expertise in interdisciplinary topics and ways to teach effectively from interdisciplinary perspectives, or creation of consortia with other campuses to share faculty expertise, facilities, and other resources.

THE EVOLVING ROLE OF DEPARTMENTS

The requirements for biology majors should be considered. Do students take courses in chemistry, physics, and mathematics departments? Do the biology faculty refer to the concepts taught in those courses in their own teaching? Do the chemistry, physics, and mathematics faculty use biological examples? Do laboratories emphasize the interdisciplinary nature of scientific research and actively make connections between disciplines? Are teaching assistants prepared to help students grasp such connections? What skills should students have when they complete their undergraduate program? Has the institution or department implemented a mechanism for measuring the success of students and faculty at reaching those goals? Designing a more interdisciplinary course of study requires answers to these questions, and the answers will often require reaching out to faculty and administrators outside of the department. In addition, it is challenging yet important to balance the needs of students with different career goals. While interdisciplinary education in biology is crucial to preparing the next generation of biomedical researchers, it also presents an opportunity to demonstrate real-world examples that will intrigue biology students. The courses and curricula proposed in Chapter 2 should help stimulate discussion among faculty as they consider their current course offering and the best ways to improve interdisciplinary learning for their students.

There are sound academic and administrative reasons for having disciplinary science departments. Disciplines attract students who then become practitioners because the students find the questions in a particular area intriguing. Successful students find the disciplines that best match their interests and individual skills. Yet faculty who teach within a discipline often are not able to make the kind of connections they hope their students can grasp. This is a major barrier to the interdisciplinary education the committee seeks to promote. Even very bright students often fail to transfer what they learn in one course to another, or to applications outside the classroom. Recent research on student learning has identified some of the key characteristics promoting learning and transfer: initial learning is essential; knowledge that is too contextualized can reduce transfer; abstraction can promote transfer; transfer is an active dynamic process; existing knowledge can sometimes lead to deep misunderstanding of new information. Departments and faculty need to utilize this educational research to guide curricular and pedagogical reform so that transfer between disciplines is promoted. This would promote immediate improvement in interdisciplinary education without need for abrupt reorganization of departments.

FACULTY

To develop an interdisciplinary approach to teaching, faculty must consider both content and pedagogy. For example, biology course content would be examined to find topics that require quantitative skills on the part of researchers. These could be examined to see how the quantitative material could be incorporated into the course, and discussion with the mathematics or other departments could ensue to see how these are being taught. This would be followed by considering, in turn, other ways that chemistry, physics, computer science, engineering, and mathematics can intersect with the topics in the course. Such changes may be difficult, but interdisciplinary teaching and interdisciplinary collaborations produce multiple benefits. Establishing partnerships with colleagues in other departments can lead to collaborations in research as well as teaching. Initial teaching of, for example, a module on the fluid dynamics of blood flow in a physiology course could be done by a colleague in physics or math. For the biology faculty, incorporating such a module would be an opportunity to learn the underlying physical science and mathematics and potentially learn the skills necessary to subsequently teach the module independently. By starting with small modules and focusing on the transfer of disciplinary material, there would be minimal change in curriculum, the biology faculty could keep the course coherent, and the students would gradually become accustomed to the teaching approach.

Further interdisciplinary teaching can be attempted by the complete restructuring of a course or the revamping of the curriculum. Successful redesign of courses and curricula (as opposed to modules) requires a much larger investment of faculty time, departmental encouragement, and significant support from the college or university administration. Faculty must master new material, delete material from preexisting courses to accommodate the new material, and adapt their teaching style to the new approach. In almost all institutions, systemic change in the curriculum lies beyond the reach of individual faculty members. In addition, sustaining change requires the creation of an institutional culture in which faculty receive appropriate support from their colleagues, department chairs, and those in control of the university budget.

REFORM INITIATIVES AND ADMINISTRATIVE SUPPORT

Colleges and universities cannot expect excellent teaching unless they actively support faculty development. Administrators need to recognize the time and effort required by encouraging faculty to take advantage of campus resources (such as teaching and learning centers and computer services) and supporting them for travel to conferences, workshops, and courses where they can learn and practice new teaching approaches and share their experiences with other faculty. As stated earlier, implanting the ideas of this report will take significant intellectual and financial resources.

For interdisciplinary education to become a reality, colleges and universities must provide incentives and help eliminate disincentives to interdepartmental collaborations. The disincentives often come about when allocation of teaching credit and the condition and organization of the physical facilities are under departmental control. Decreasing barriers and increasing communication between departments will require mechanisms that facilitate faculty teaching out-of-department courses. These will often require increasing the recognition and rewards for faculty who teach outside of their department, possibly by allocating credit hours for teaching based on the department of the faculty member instead of the department listing the course. Interdisciplinary innovation also will require substantial faculty time and effort to develop new course materials, adapt existing curricula to their particular needs,[1] and learn new topics. Departments and colleges must find new ways to make these resources available to help faculty and to recognize and reward their efforts. Again, departmental structures must evolve to meet these new needs.

At many institutions, graduate teaching assistants also play an important educational role. They must receive more preparation for their teach-

---

[1]The National Science Foundation's Division of Undergraduate Education now offers support to faculty who seek to adopt and adapt existing modules and curricula to their own circumstances. This Adaptation and Implementation program is a component of the long-established Course, Curriculum, and Laboratory Improvement initiative. For additional information: *http://www.ehr.nsf.gov/ehr/DUE/programs/ccli/*

ing mission, especially when assisting in novel interdisciplinary courses. The Preparing Future Faculty initiative, a joint effort of the Council of Graduate Schools and the Association of American Colleges and Universities, offers insights on how to provide graduate students with this kind of experience. Preparing Future Faculty can also help current faculty consider how student learning might vary from discipline to discipline. Additional information is available at: *http://www.preparing-faculty.org/*. Both faculty and TAs need to learn new subject matter and new pedagogical approaches to teaching and enhancing learning across disciplines.

FACILITIES

A major constraint on increasing interdisciplinary education is the physical layout of the teaching facilities. The science teaching spaces on most campuses today are typically located in buildings constructed in the immediate post-Sputnik era when the U.S. government was promoting science as a way to "catch up" with the Soviets. These old spaces reflect the strong influence of the inflexible, discipline-oriented laboratory spaces of that era and are ill suited for new pedagogical approaches and the presentation of interdisciplinary science necessary to train the life scientists of the future. Laboratories were often designed in ways that make student-student interactions challenging (i.e., floor-to-ceiling lab benches and shelves). Many institutions are now planning and building new science teaching and research facilities, or renovating old ones. Planning such teaching and research space provides a unique opportunity for any institution to seek answers to the fundamental questions about how space can be arranged to optimize educational objectives. An understanding of, and focus upon, the curriculum to be taught and the learning objectives to be realized must serve as the foundation upon which new or renovated spaces are designed. Integration of curricular mission and focus, along with overall space needs, is essential before any institution can identify what kind of facilities are required for its programs. Teaching and research facilities must be designed and developed to work synergistically with new, interdisciplinary pedagogical approaches and to emulate the physical environments in which students will ultimately work. An invaluable resource to help faculty and administrators with this design and planning process is *Project Kaleidoscope Volume III, Structures for Science: A Handbook on Planning Facilities for Undergraduate Natural Science Communities* .

NATIONAL NETWORKS FOR REFORM

Transformation of the undergraduate biology currculum is tied to issues that extend beyond the reach of a single campus. Issues related to faculty rewards, recognition, respect, and promotion and tenure are national in scope. Many individuals, institutions, organizations, and informal networks are working to address these issues. Many disciplinary societies have education committees that address undergraduate teaching. Some, such as the American Society for Microbiology (ASM), employ full-time staff to make these efforts more successful. ASM holds two education meetings annually, one focused on faculty and the other on undergraduates themselves. Other groups devoted to undergraduate education in biology are less formal. The Association of College & University Biology Educators (ACUBE) was first established in 1957 as the Association of Midwest College Biology Teachers, but now tries to attract more nationwide participation. ACUBE works to improve the teaching of the biological sciences, identify common problems involving biological curricula, encourage active participation in biological research by teachers and students in the belief that such participation is an invaluable adjunct to effective teaching, and create a collective voice for teachers of the biological sciences. Additional information is available at *http://www.acube.org/*.

One group with a national reach is Project Kaleidoscope (PKAL). PKAL members include faculty from all types of colleges and universities and all disciplines of the sciences. An important feature of PKAL is that participants in disciplinary and interdisciplinary workshops leave with specific action plans to implement on their home campus. Project Kaleidoscope has worked since 1989 to identify and disseminate sound principles and methods on which to base undergraduate education in the natural sciences and mathematics. The PKAL reform movement has used a multidisciplinary approach, bringing scientists from many disciplines together to work through common issues. It operates by looking for "what works" and encouraging others to apply those approaches in their own teaching. PKAL is currently focusing on the importance of institutional change and building design in educational reform. Its meetings, workshops, and institutes have helped to break down some of the barriers between chemists and biologists, particularly among the younger generation of faculty involved in PKAL's Faculty for the 21st Century. This initiative provides support for young professors who have been recognized by their academic deans as emerging education leaders by linking them with similar faculty at other institutions. PKAL also has significant experience in addressing the question of how to effect change, and its strategy focuses on promoting reform at the grassroots. Additional information is available at *http://pkal.org.*

NURTURING THE PRODUCTION OF NEW BOOKS AND OTHER TEACHING MATERIALS

As was discussed earlier, the transformation of undergraduate biology education is critically dependent on the availability of new texts and monographs, project-based laboratory guides and materials, and modules to enhance interdisciplinary education. The potential formats of these needed teaching materials are diverse and complementary: printed books and guides, CDs and videos, Web sites, and interactive computer programs. The most effective and influential teaching materials arise from the creative activity of committed scientists and educators. This is an exciting and rapidly changing area not only because of the evolving combinations of textbooks, computerized materials, labs and simulation programs, but also because of the changing roles of commercial publishers, software developers, and nonprofit institutions and organizations.

To facilitate the design and production of these materials, individual colleges and universities must support these efforts. They do not necessarily need to provide the financial support that could come from other sources. However, faculty members will need to devote considerable time to conduct background research and to ensure that content is appropriate and accessible. Faculty also need time and resources to prepare new teaching materials or to find ways to adopt and adapt existing materials to their particular circumstances. Colleges and universities should provide sabbaticals and release time in the form of defined periods of reduced professional responsibilities (teaching, service, or research) to enable prospective authors to concentrate on such development work. Educational institutions, foundations, and publishing companies can encourage and catalyze innovative authoring in many ways. The development of teaching materials requires computer and visualization resources, and staff or students who are knowledgeable in their use in order to fully develop new teaching concepts and approaches. The design and promotion of the new materials can be greatly enhanced by consulting professionals in graphics or marketing. Private foundations can play a key role by financing these types of resources and also by sponsoring new works while they are still in their early stages of development, particularly those that do not conform to what publishers perceive as fitting into the current marketplace. Publishers will step in when proof-of-principle is established. Foundations can help initiate innovative new projects and bring them to the point of commercial viability. Web sites can also play a valuable role in making interdisciplinary topics accessible to both faculty and students, and their role seems likely to grow in the future.

Second, professional societies and other national organizations can play a major role in furthering the creation of new teaching materials. They have a keen sense of the cutting edge of their disciplines. They also possess the stature to bring together prospective authors from different institutions and to enter into partnerships with publishing companies to produce and market new works (e.g., the American Chemical Society's current development of a new general chemistry text). Third, a wealth of teaching material exists on the Internet, but information about the quality and effectiveness of most of it is not readily accessible. Too much time can be spent in searching for the right video or in deciphering a program or set of data in order to use it in the classroom. Highly selective and curated Internet sites for educational purposes are needed, such as the National Science, Technology, Engineering, and Mathematics Education Digital Library being developed by the National Science Foundation.[2] Simple uniform graphical user interfaces would help greatly in furthering the extensive and facile use of these wonderful resources. The scientific community also could increase the attractiveness of authorship by honoring faculty who have created innovative educational works. Such awards would call attention to the best new materials and highlight their value to educational institutions.

FINANCIAL SUPPORT FOR IMPROVING UNDERGRADUATE BIOLOGY EDUCATION

The reform of undergraduate biology education is a complex task that will require substantial financial resources. Curriculum development, as-

---

[2]The National STEM Education Digital Library program (NSDL) project is composing digital libraries in multiple scientific disciplines in order to facilitate the online sharing of learning environments and resources for STEM education. The digital library will serve as an effective way to hold a large compilation of STEM educational research and tools in a structured manner to facilitate easy access to its contents. Additional information is available at *http://www.ehr.nsf.gov/ehr/DUE/programs/nsdl/*.

sessment and evaluation, sustainable change, and faculty development all entail costs. In most cases, only a limited amount of those resources will come from the individual college or university. The two principal organizations that have funded undergraduate biology education are NSF and HHMI.

NSF supports a diverse array of projects in undergraduate science education. These projects fund activities such as research by undergraduates. One example is the REU programs in which each student is assigned to a specific research project and works together with faculty, postdocs, and graduate students for one summer. Other programs include faculty research at primarily undergraduate institutions (RUI), curricular reform, design of materials for assessment, and dissemination of information across the country. NSF has begun awarding the title of Distinguished Teaching Scholar to a small number of faculty members who have contributed greatly to science, technology, engineering, and mathematics (STEM) education. One of the goals of the program is to increase the recruitment of other faculty to work on science education. The program aims to reward individuals who have contributed to the scholarship of STEM education, and also hold an exemplary record of instructing undergraduates. In the first two rounds of awards, announced in November 2001 and May 2002, no biologists were named as Distinguished Teaching Scholars.

The Centers of Learning and Teaching (CLT) are multiyear grants to consortia of individuals and organizations that develop and implement research-based programs to address the issues and needs of the STEM instructional workforce. They design and implement new approaches to assessment, research on learning, curriculum and materials development, and research-based instruction. Originally the centers focused only on K-12 education, but NSF now plans to fund two centers that focus on postsecondary education. NSF also supports the Chautauqua series of summer faculty development courses.

Another area of effort for NSF is programs designed to increase understanding of how students learn. Research on Learning and Education (ROLE) supports research into the brain and behavioral, cognitive, affective, and social aspects of human learning, as well as research on STEM learning in formal and informal settings. The Assessment of Student Achievement in Undergraduate Education (ASA) program supports the development and distribution of materials on the effectiveness of courses, curricula, programs of study, and academic institutions that promote STEM learning. ASA supports the development of new assessment tools, the adaptation of assessment materials, and the dissemination of effective assessment practices through workshops and web-based learning. The Course, Curriculum, and Laboratory Improvement (CCLI) program attempts to improve STEM education through changes in learning environments, course content, curricula, and educational practices. The program has three tracks. First, Educational Material Development focuses on producing new, innovative materials, such as textbooks, that incorporate effective learning practices in order to enhance student comprehension in STEM. Second, the National Dissemination project seeks to provide faculty members with development opportunities, such as workshops, in order to implement effective educational practices as well as improve the quality of their teaching. Finally, adaptation and implementation projects aim to improve STEM education by implementing previously tested and developed educational practices into the curricula of STEM. (More discussion of this project is found in footnote 2 in this chapter.)

The federal government is not the only source of funding for projects in undergraduate biology education. Private institutions play a crucial role, most notably the Howard Hughes Medical Institute. HHMI invested more than $476 million between 1987 and 2001 to support improvements in biology education at 232 colleges and universities. Their investment has transformed biology instruction at these institutions, in ways ranging from developing new curricula, hiring new faculty, promoting faculty development, and supporting independent research by undergraduate students. Many examples of outstanding programs can be found on their Web site and in publications (such as *Beyond Bio 101*), including examples of integration of science teaching across disciplines, especially at small colleges. The institute also has recently launched the HHMI Professors program to honor and support faculty who provide leadership in undergraduate education. The first awards were made in the fall of 2002 to biologists with excellent credentials in both teaching and research.

One foundation that has had a major impact in building an interdisciplinary approach is the Whitaker Foundation. Whitaker funds projects to enhance research and education in biomedical engineering in the United States and Canada. Biomedical engineering combines computer and engineering technology with the study of complex biological systems, and is an inherently interdisciplinary field. Departments of biomedical engineering draw faculty from many different disciplines. Established in 1975 by U.A. Whitaker, the foundation has already dispensed $600 million and will spend down its endowment to completely phase out its operations by 2006.

Whitaker (*www.whitaker.org*) supports a variety of programs including faculty research (300 projects), creation or expansion of departments of biomedical engineering, fellowships for graduate students (180 students), internships in industry and at NIH (120 programs), creation of teaching materials and conferences, and workshops in biomedical engineering. The foundation has recently consolidated a number of initiatives into Leadership and Development Awards that provide substantial funding to institutions committed to continuing to build up biomedical engineering after the foundation closes its doors.

The foundation held a Biomedical Engineering Educational Summit in December 2000 that brought together 123 institutions from the United States and Canada and 24 overseas institutions (*http://summit.whitaker.org*). It was designed to review the wide variety of interdisciplinary programs receiving Whitaker support. The summit participants did not agree on one unique curriculum that would suit all schools because each institution has molded its biomedical engineering program to its mission and the needs of its faculty and students. The summit highlighted the fact that like other engineering programs, those in biomedical engineering frequently incorporate real-world problems and tasks into their curricula. Most of the departments emphasize critical thinking, teamwork, interpersonal skills, group decisions, analysis and problem-solving processes, and oral and written communication skills in their courses. Biomedical engineering laboratories are designed to incorporate equipment and procedures that are common in the workplace. In many cases, computer simulations are used when the actual procedures cannot be carried out. The development of biomedical engineering over the past decade demonstrates that a focused effort, such as that undertaken by the Whitaker Foundation, has the potential to catalyze the growth of a new interdisciplinary field, both in terms of its research and its educational curriculum.

HARMONIZING THE UNDERGRADUATE SCIENCE EDUCATION OF FUTURE GRADUATE STUDENTS AND MEDICAL STUDENTS

RECOMMENDATION #7

Medical school admissions requirements and the Medical College Admissions Test (MCAT) are hindering change in the undergraduate biology curriculum and should be reexamined in light of the recommendations in this report.

Innovation in undergraduate biology education is constrained by medical school admission requirements and specifically by the MCAT exam. The committee recommends that an independent review of medical school admission requirements and testing be conducted in light of the rapidly changing nature of biological and biomedical research, and the consequent need to transform undergraduate science education.

The curricular demands placed on undergraduate programs by students who want to score well on the Medical College Admission Test (MCAT) have a major impact on the curriculum and course content of all life science majors, especially at schools where the same courses are offered to premeds and those headed for research careers. This is especially true of the chemistry courses taken by the majority of life science majors. Most medical schools in the United States require applicants to have completed one year of general chemistry and one year of organic chemistry. In addition, satisfactory performance on the MCAT is a key admission requirement for medical school. Changes that would likely benefit both groups of students are limited by the need to prepare premedical students for medical school admission committees and the current format of the MCAT itself, although it is by no means clear that the current testing regime is particularly relevant to preparing future physicians of the 21st century. Indeed, premedical students constitute a substantial proportion of the next generation of biomedical researchers who will need to be leaders in the same dynamically changing landscape of biomedical research as life science majors. Medicine itself is becoming more interdisciplinary, and future physicians could also benefit from the interdisciplinary changes called for in this report.

A change in the MCAT itself, or in the way it is used for medical school admissions, would allow the biology curriculum to develop in a way that is beneficial to all students instead of allowing the content of the MCAT to dictate what students are taught.

THE CENTRAL ROLE OF FACULTY DEVELOPMENT IN CURRICULUM TRANSFORMATION

Undergraduate biology education can be effectively transformed only through close and sustained collaboration between colleges, universities, government agencies, professional societies, and foundations. It is often assumed that once a useful pedagogical approach is identified, it will be reproducible, easy to disseminate, and simple for another faculty member to implement in his/her home institution. The reality is that in teaching, as in research, faculty need to be trained to carry out new tasks and their efforts to do so need to be recognized. *Investing in Faculty,* a recent Project Kaleidoscope report, comments on the importance of faculty development and presents "An Investment Roadmap" describing ways institutions can enhance teaching (PKAL, 2000). *Making Teaching Community Property* focuses more on actions by faculty, including mentoring of new faculty, team teaching, and collaborative approaches to inquiry. A historical perspective on faculty responsibilities is presented in *Scholarship Reconsidered: Priorities of the Professorate* .

RECOMMENDATION #8

Faculty development is a crucial component to improving undergraduate biology education. Efforts must be made on individual campuses and nationally to provide faculty the time necessary to refine their own understanding of how the integrative relationships of biology, mathematics, and the physical sciences can be best melded into either existing courses or new courses in the particular areas of science in which they teach.

The committee recommends the creation of a new venue to promote discussion, analyze outcomes, and sustain innovation in the reform of undergraduate biology education. An annual summer institute dedicated to faculty development for biology professors (and other science faculty as appropriate) would be an effective and appropriate means of building on the ideas of Bio2010 and fostering continued innovation in biology education.

The institute that the committee proposes would be modeled after the Cold Spring Harbor summer courses, which played a historic role in the shaping of modern biology. Those courses provide a seamless combination of presentations, discussions, and experiments, with students (faculty, postdocs, and graduate students), instructors, and visiting speakers living together on the grounds. The sharing of data, ideas, and methods is a continuum that takes place in the lab, over meals, and during social interludes. The community that grew out of this intimate and intensive learning environment helped give birth to molecular biology as a scientific discipline. A comparable institute for biology education would help nurture the growth of a similar kind of community. Success would require a long-term commitment to the project and sufficient staff to facilitate the efforts of faculty during the fall, winter, and spring.

A summer institute for biology education would be a venue for faculty to share information and experiences. It would help to increase communication between research universities and primarily undergraduate institutions by bringing faculty from both types of institutions together to learn from each other. It would facilitate the development, adaptation, and dissemination of innovative courses and course materials while providing training workshops for faculty and encouraging the development of a community of scientists/educators. The institute would promote a better integration of research and education at the research universities while giving teaching institutions better access to leading-edge research. The courses and workshops taught at the institute would consider pedagogical approaches and teaching materials as well as the overall content and architecture of courses and curricula. Discussions of how to adapt the ideas to fit other scientific topics, course structures, and institutions would be a major component of each workshop. Given the heterogeneity of the U.S. system of higher education, no single model is broadly applicable. One of the most important aspects of such summer courses is that the participants would learn how to develop necessary course elements and adapt them to their own institutions and students. At the same time, the courses would help to build a community of biologists dedicated to creating new ways for students to learn biology. This community would facilitate the transfer of knowledge back to their home campuses and within the disciplinary societies of which they are members. They would remain linked to the summer institute community as members of a virtual network, at follow-up meetings, and via an Internet meeting place.

Potential Topics for Summer Institute Workshops Include the Following:

• Development of modules and detailed guides to narrow topics suitable for incorporating into existing courses. Potential areas for modules are the integration of quantitative examples into biology courses, or the presentation of examples from recent biological research that rely upon basic principles of chemistry or physics.

• Design of new courses that expose students to the excitement of modern biology such as seminars that include both student projects and presentations on faculty research.

• Ideas for exposing large numbers of students to research (how to think like a scientist): from laboratory courses to computer simulations to conceptual experiments.

• Development of teaching materials for the sharing of innovative modules, courses, and conceptual experiments.

• Approaches to interdisciplinary courses including team teaching and modules.

• Approaches on how to incorporate recently emerging research about how people learn into designing curricula and evaluating student learning, such as that presented in *How People Learn* (NRC, 1999a) and *Knowing What Students Know* .

A successful institute would require a sincere partnership among a variety of intitutions and organizations. A collaboration between the NAS, NRC, HHMI, and NSF would help to anchor the effort in the research establishment. Cooperation with disciplinary societies in biology would also be pursued, and the institute would take advantage of work done by Project Kaleidoscope and groups funded by HHMI, as well as NSF and any other government agencies. The institute would provide a mechanism for building on those efforts and promote faculty development for professors at all stages in their careers. A successful collaboration would also expand the possibilities for further disseminating the work that comes out of the summer institute. For example, follow-up meetings could be held at the annual meetings of disciplinary societies to spread the word to faculty unable to attend the previous summer's institute and to attract new participants for the next summer.

A series of planning meetings has already begun with representatives of the above groups. The current draft proposal calls for an initial workshop on designing interdisciplinary modules for existing courses and recommends an oversight committee to determine future workshops, select instructors, provide continuity, assess the impact of the workshops, and set overall policy and direction. One goal of the institute would be to bring research into the curriculum. Efforts would be made to attract research faculty to the institute in order to facilitate that goal. Preliminary information indicates that research-oriented faculty would participate in such workshops if it were to benefit them professionally and make it easier for them to fulfill their teaching responsibilities (Lillian Tong, Center for Biology Education, University of Wisconsin-Madison, personal communication, April 2002). A summer institute that is well grounded in the scientific establishment would improve faculty contacts with respected members of the research community and provide a mechanism for faculty to acquire the conceptual and practical skills necessary for quality teaching and learning.

Future biomedical researchers will require not only expertise in a specific biological system, but a conceptual understanding of the science of life and where a specific research topic fits into the overall picture. Connections between biology and the other scientific disciplines need to be developed and reinforced so that interdisciplinary thinking and work become second nature. Teaching and learning must be made more active to engage undergraduates, fully prepare them for graduate study, and give them an enduring sense of the power and beauty of creative inquiry. For these changes to happen colleges and universities must reexamine their current curricula. Administrators, funding agencies, and professional societies should all work to encourage the collaboration of faculty in different departments and the development of teaching materials that incorporate mathematics, physical science, or information science into a biology education. There must be rewards for faculty who create, assess, and sustain new educational programs. Faculty must feel encouraged to spend the time necessary to dedicate themselves to the task of understanding the integrative relationships of biology, mathematics, and the physical sciences, and how they can communicate these relationships to their students.

7

References

American Association for Higher Education Teaching Initiative. (1993). *Preparing Graduate Students to Teach: A Guide to Programs That Improve Undergraduate Education and Develop Tomorrow's Faculty.* Washington, DC: American Association for Higher Education.

American Cancer Society, Burroughs Wellcome Fund, and Howard Hughes Medical Institute. (2000). *The Role of the Private Sector in Training the Next Generation of Biomedical Scientists.* Proceedings of a conference held at HHMI in February 2000. Chevy Chase, MD: Howard Hughes Medical Institute.

Berg, H. C. (1993). *Random Walks in Biology.* Princeton, NJ: Princeton University Press.

Boyer, E. L. (1990). *Scholarship Reconsidered: Priorities of the Professoriate.* New York: Carnegie Foundation for the Advancement of Teaching.

Brunet, M. et al. (2002, July). A new hominid from the Upper Miocine of Chad, Central Africa. *Nature, 418,* 145-151.

Cavalli-Sforza, L. L. (2000). *Genes, People, and Languages.* New York: North Point Press.

Coalition for Education in the Life Sciences, University of Wisconsin-Madison. (1992). *Issues-Based Framework for Bio 101 from the Report of the National Life Science Education Conference II, February 21-23, 1992.* Madison, WI: Author.

Coalition for Education in the Life Sciences, University of Wisconsin-Madison. (1998). *Professional Societies and the Faculty Scholar: Promoting Scholarship and Learning in the Life Sciences.* Madison, WI: Author.

Davis, B. G. (1993). *Tools for Teaching.* San Francisco: Jossey-Bass.

Denny, M. W. (1993). *Air and Water: The Biology and Physics of Life's Media.* Princeton, NJ: Princeton University Press.

Doyle, M. P. (Ed.). (2000). *Academic Excellence: The Role of Research in the Physical Sciences at Undergraduate Institutions.* Tempe, AZ: Research Corporation.

Edelstein-Keshet, L. (1988). *Mathematical Models in Biology.* Boston: Birkhauser Publishing.

Feynman, R. P., Leighton, R. B., and Sands, M. L. (1963). *The Feynman Lectures on Physics.* Reading, MA; London: Addison-Wesley.

Hakim, T. M. (2000). *How To Develop and Administer Institutional Undergraduate Research Programs.* Washington, DC: Council on Undergraduate Research.

Hartl, D. L. and Clark, A. G. (1997). *Principles of Population Dynamics* (3rd ed.). Sunderland, MA: Sinauer Associates.

Hille, B. (2001). *Ionic Channels of Excitable Membranes* (3rd ed.). Sunderland, MA: Sinauer Associates.

Hoppensteadt, F. C. and Peskin C. S. (1992). *Mathematics in Medicine and the Life Sciences.* New York: Springer Publishing.

Howard, J. (2001). *Mechanics of Motor Proteins and the Cytoskeleton.* Sunderland, MA: Sinauer Associates.

Howard Hughes Medical Institute. (2001). *HHMI Annual Report 2000.* Chevy Chase, MD: Author.

Hutchings, P. (1996). *Making Teaching Community Property: A Menu for Peer Collaboration and Peer Review.* Washington, DC: American Association for Higher Education.

Kenny, R. W. and Boyer Commission on Educating Undergraduates in the Research University. (1998). *Reinventing Undergraduate Education: A Blueprint for America's Research Universities.* Stony Brook: State University of New York.

Laws, P. W. (1997). *Workshop Physics Activity Guide.* New York: John Wiley & Sons.

Marocco, D. A. (2000). Biology for the 21st Century: The Search for a Core. *The American Biology Teacher* 62(8), 565-569.

Mazur, E. (1997). *Peer Instruction: A User's Manual.* Upper Saddle River, NJ: Prentice Hall, Inc.

McNeal, A. P. and D'Avanzo, C. (1997). *Student-Active Science: Models of Innovation in College Science Teaching.* Proceedings on the NSF Sponsored Conference on Inquiry Approaches to Science Teaching Held at Hampshire College, June 1996. Fort Worth, TX: Saunders College Publishing.

Murray, J. D. (1993). *Mathematical Biology* (2nd ed.). New York: Springer Publishing.

National Institute of General Medical Sciences and National Science Foundation. Joint DMS/NIGMS Initiative to Support Research Grants in the Area of Mathematical Biology. Available at: http://www.nsf.gov/pubs/2002/nsf02125/nsf02125.htm [August 16, 2002].

National Research Council. (1996). *From Analysis to Action: Undergraduate Education in Science, Mathematics, Engineering, and Technology.* Report of a Convocation. Center for Science, Mathematics, and Engineering Education. Washington, DC: National Academy Press.

National Research Council. (1997a). *Adviser, Teacher, Role Model, Friend: On Being a Mentor to Students in Science and Engineering.* Committee on Science, Engineering, and Public Policy. Washington, DC: National Academy Press.

National Research Council. (1997b). *Science Teaching Reconsidered: A Handbook.* Committee on Undergraduate Science Education. Center for Science, Mathematics, and Engineering Education. Washington, DC: National Academy Press.

National Research Council. (1998). *A Strategy for Research in Space Biology and Medicine into the Next Century.* Committee on Space Biology in Medicine. Washington, DC: National Academy Press.

National Research Council. (1999a). *How People Learn: Brain, Mind, Experience, and School.* Committee on Developments in the Science of Learning. Commission on Behavioral and Social Sciences and Education. Washington, DC: National Academy Press.

National Research Council. (1999b). *Transforming Undergraduate Education in Science, Mathematics, Engineering, and Technology.* Committee on Undergraduate Science Education. Center for Science, Mathematics, and Engineering Education. Washington, DC: National Academy Press.

National Research Council. (2000a). *Addressing the Nation's Changing Needs for Biomedical and Behavioral Scientists.* Committee on National Needs for Biomedical and Behavioral Scientists, Education and Career Studies Unit. Washington, DC: National Academy Press.

National Research Council. (2000b). *From Monsoons to Microbes: Understanding the Ocean's Role in Human Health.* Committee on the Ocean's Role in Human Health. Division on Earth and Life Studies. Washington, DC: National Academy Press.

National Research Council. (2000c). *Inquiry and the National Science Education Standards: A Guide for Teaching and Learning.* Committee on the Development of an Addendum to the National Science Education Standards on Scientific Inquiry. Washington, DC: National Academy Press.

National Research Council. (2000d). *The Aging Mind: Opportunities in Cognitive Research.* Committee on Future Directions for Cognitive Research on Aging. Board on Behavioral, Cognitive, and Sensory Sciences. Washington, DC: National Academy Press.

National Research Council. (2001a). *Cells and Surveys: Should Biological Measures Be Included in Social Science Research?* Committee on Population. Division of Behavioral and Social Sciences and Education. Washington, DC: National Academy Press.

National Research Council. (2001b). *Health and Behavior: The Interplay of Biological, Behavioral, and Societal Influences.* Committee on Health and Behavior: Research, Practice, and Policy. Board on Neuroscience and Behavioral Health. Washington, DC: National Academy Press.

National Research Council. (2001c). *Knowing What Students Know.* Committee on the Foundations of Assessment. Center for Education. Washington, DC: National Academy Press.

National Research Council. (2002). *Learning and Understanding: Improving Advanced Study of Mathematics and Science in U.S. High Schools.* Committee on Programs for Advanced Study in Mathematics and Science. Washington, DC: National Academy Press.

National Science Foundation. (2000). Integrative Graduate Education and Research Traineeship (IGERT) Program. Available at: *http://www.nsf.gov/home/crssprgm/igert/start.htm* [August 16, 2002].

National Science Foundation and National Science Board. (2000). *Science and Engineering Indicators 2000.* Arlington, VA: National Science Foundation.

O'Donnell, A., DuRussel, L., and Derry, S. (1997). *Cognitive Processes in Interdisciplinary Groups: Problems and Possibilities.* Research Monograph No. 5. Madison: National Institute for Science Education, University of Wisconsin–Madison.

Project Kaleidoscope. (1995). *Structures for Science: A Handbook on Planning Facilities for Undergraduate Natural Science Communities.* Washington, DC: Author.

Project Kaleidoscope. (2000). *Investing in Faculty.* Washington, DC: Author.

Research Corporation and Doyle, M. P. (Eds.). (2000). *Academic Excellence: The Role of Research in the Physical Sciences at Undergraduate Institutions.* Tucson, AZ: Research Corporation.

Rothman, F. G. and Narum, J. L. (1999). *Then, Now, and In the Next Decade: A Commentary on Strengthening Undergraduate Science, Mathematics, Engineering and Technology Education.* Washington, DC: Project Kaleidoscope.

Seymour, E. and Hewitt, N. M. (1997). *Talking About Leaving: Why Undergraduates Leave the Sciences.* Boulder, CO: Westview Press.

Siebert, E. D. and McIntosh, W. J. (2001). *College Pathways to the Science Education Standards.* Arlington, VA: National Science Teachers Association.

Sigma Xi, The Scientific Research Society. (2000). *Reshaping Undergraduate Science and Engineering Education: Tools for Better Learning.* Research Triangle Park, NC: Author.

Springer, L., Stanne, M. E., and Donova, S. S. (1997). *Effects of Small-Group Learning on Undergraduates in Science, Mathematics, Engineering, and Technology: A Meta-Analysis.* Research Monograph No. 11. Madison: National Institute for Science Education, University of Wisconsin-Madison.

Taubes, C. H. (2001). *Modeling Differential Equations in Biology.* Upper Saddle River, NJ: Prentice-Hall Publishing.

Tobias, S. and Raphael, J. (1977). *The Hidden Curriculum—Faculty-Made Tests in Science: Part 1 Lower-Division Courses.* New York: Plenum Publishing Corporation.

University of British Columbia. (1996). Science First! series ready to ignite students' curiosity. *UBC Reports* 42.

University of California, Los Angeles, Higher Education Research Institute, and Cooperative Institutional Research Program. (2001). *The American Freshman: National Norms for Fall 2001.* Los Angeles: Higher Education Research Institute.

Uno, G. E. (1997). *Handbook on Teaching Undergraduate Science Courses: A Survival Training Manual.* Thompson Custom Publishing.

U.S. Department of Education, National Institute for Science Education, and Adelman, C. (1998). *Women and Men of the Engineering Path: A Model for Analyses of Undergraduate Careers.* Washington, DC: U.S. Government Printing Office.

Vogel, S. (1998). *Cats' Paws and Catapults: Mechanical Worlds of Nature and People.* New York: W.W. Norton & Company.

Appendixes

A

Charge to the Committee

The project will examine the formal undergraduate education, training, and experience required to prepare the next generation of life scientists. An important goal of the project is to identify fundamental skills in mathematics, chemistry, physics, computer science, and engineering that could be integrated into an undergraduate major in the life sciences to assist future scientists in making novel interdisciplinary connections. The report will emphasize preparing students for biomedical research, but will also evaluate preparation for other life science disciplines such as plant biology, population and evolutionary biology, and behavior and cognitive sciences. Case studies will be generated to provide suggestions for implementing reforms at both universities and four-year colleges.

Specific subjects to be addressed in the study will include:

1. How will biology research be conducted in the future?

2. What fundamental skills and knowledge are needed by undergraduates to prepare them to excel as biological research scientists?

3. How are those skills and knowledge best conveyed? What are reasonable objectives for undergraduate education?

4. What elements of mathematics, chemistry, physics, computer science, and engineering will assist students in making novel interdisciplinary connections?

5. To what extent can these skills and knowledge be taught in the context of central issues in biology?

6. Should these skills and concepts be acquired through a restructuring of biology courses or through a broadening of the content and structure of courses in mathematics, chemistry, and physics?

7. To the extent that portions of the desired curriculum are better treated in academic departments outside the life sciences, what are the best practices for collaborating with faculty in those departments to achieve mutually agreeable goals?

8. What institutional barriers to collaboration exist and how have they been addressed in successful cases of curricular change? What incentives exist or might be created to overcome barriers to change?

9. What innovative programs for teaching life science majors have been developed, and what can be learned from those programs?

B

Biographical Information on Committee Members

Lubert Stryer, *Chair*, is the Winzer Professor in the School of Medicine and professor of neurobiology at Stanford University. He recently served as chairman and chief scientific officer of Senomyx, Inc., a chemosensory technologies biotech company in La Jolla, California. His research in neurobiology has focused on vision and calcium signaling. Among his many honors, he is a member of the National Academy of Sciences, a Fellow of the American Academy of Arts and Sciences, and recipient of the AAAS Newcomb Cleveland Prize and the Distinguished Inventors Award from the Intellectual Property Owners Association. He has taught biochemistry, biophysics, cell biology, and neurobiology, and has authored four editions of a textbook on biochemistry. He received a BS from the University of Chicago and an MD from Harvard University.

Ronald Breslow is a University Professor and professor of chemistry and professor of biology at Columbia University. His research in bioorganic and physical organic chemistry includes the development of novel molecules and artificial enzymes. He is a former president of the American Chemical Society and was named "one of the top 75 contributors to the chemical enterprise in the past 75 years" in a 1997 poll conducted by Chemical and Engineering News. Among his many honors are the National Medal of Science and the Priestley Medal. He holds membership in the National Academy of Sciences, the American Philosophical Society, the

American Academy of Arts and Sciences, the Royal Society of Great Britain, and the Royal Society of Chemistry of London, as well as honorary membership in the Indian Academy of Sciences and the Japanese Chemical Society. He received the Columbia University Great Teacher Award and the Mark van Doren Medal for teaching, also awarded by Columbia University. He has BS and PhD degrees in chemistry from Harvard University, as well as a master's in medical science, also from Harvard.

James Gentile is dean for the natural sciences at Hope College in Holland, Michigan. His research focuses on the connection between inflammation and cancer. He is currently editor-in-chief for the journal *Mutation Research*. He has received the Cancer Research Medallion from the National Cancer Institute of Japan, among other awards. He has served as a member of the Science Advisory Board for the U.S. Environmental Protection Agency. He is a former president of the Environmental Mutagen Society, which awarded him the Student Educator of the Year Award in 1998. He is a past council member of the Council on Undergraduate Research. He also serves on the executive committee for Project Kaleidoscope. He is currently serving on the NRC's Committee on Undergraduate Education. He has been program director for grants from HHMI, NSF, and the W.M. Keck Foundation to improve undergraduate science education at Hope College. His bachelor's degree is from St. Mary's University in Minnesota and PhD from Illinois State University.

David M. Hillis is director of the School of Biological Sciences and Roark Centennial Professor in the Section of Integrative Biology and the Institute of Cellular and Molecular Biology at the University of Texas at Austin. His research is on the evolution of biotic diversity and uses the techniques of molecular genetics to study relationships among populations, species, and higher taxa. He received the NSF Presidential Young Investigator Award in 1987 and the MacArthur Fellowship in 1999. He is a past president of the Society of Systematic Biologists, president of the Society for the Study of Evolution, and a member of the American Academy of Arts and Sciences. He received his undergraduate degree from Baylor University and a PhD in biological sciences from the University of Kansas.

John Hopfield is Howard A. Prior Professor in the Life Sciences and professor of molecular biology at Princeton University. His research encompasses neurobiology and computing networks. He is a member of the National Academy of Sciences, American Academy of Arts and Sciences, and American Philosophical Society. He has received the MacArthur Fellowship and the APS prize in Biophysics, and was named California Scientist of the Year for 1991. He has taught in physics departments (from first-year physics to graduate condensed matter physics), in chemistry departments (first-year chemistry to graduate biophysical chemistry), and now in a molecular biology department, where he teaches a senior course related to how networks of neuron-like elements compute. He has a bachelor's degree from Swarthmore College and PhD from Cornell University.

Nancy Kopell is W.G. Aurelio Professor of Mathematics and Science and co-director of the Center for BioDynamics (a multidisciplinary center for biology, mathematics, and engineering) at Boston University. Her research includes the mathematics of self-organizing systems (both physical and biological); currently she is focusing on dynamics of the nervous system, especially rhythmic activity associated with cognition and motor control. She was awarded a MacArthur Fellowship and is a member of the National Academy of Sciences. She received a bachelor's degree from Cornell University and PhD from University of California at Berkeley.

Sharon Long is dean of the School of Humanities and Sciences and professor of biological sciences at Stanford University. Her research examines the interaction of Rhizobium bacteria with a host plant in symbiotic nitrogen fixation. She is a member of the National Academy of Sciences, and a Fellow of the American Academy of Arts and Sciences. She served on the NRC Committee on Undergraduate Science Education from 1993-1996. At Stanford she served on departmental and university committees for curriculum development. She teaches departmental courses in biochemistry, molecular biology, and genetics and helped design and teach an interdisciplinary course for nonmajors on Light in the Physical and Biological World. Her undergraduate degree is from California Institute of Technology and her PhD is from Yale University.

Edward Penhoet is director for science and higher education programs at the Gordon and Betty Moore Foundation. He was previously dean of the School of Public Health at the University of California at Berkeley. He co-founded Chiron and was president and CEO until 1998. He has published extensively on biochemistry of viruses and vertebrates. He was a member of the NRC Committee on Undergraduate Science Education from 1998 to

1999 and served on the NRC committee that recently produced the report *Addressing the Nation's Changing Needs for Biomedical and Behavioral Scientists*. He has served as a member of the NIH Economic Roundtable on Biomedical Research and the Board of National Foundation for Biomedical Research of the NIH, and as chair for the NIH Forum on Sponsored Research Agreements. He was a member of the University of California (system-wide) Biotechnology Advisory Committee. He is on the board of directors for the Foundation for California Community Colleges. While at Chiron, he continued to teach undergraduates at Berkeley, including a biochemistry course. He received Berkeley's first Distinguished Faculty Award for the Department of Molecular and Cell Biology in 1991 and was also awarded a Dreyfus Foundation Teacher-Scholar Award. His bachelor's degree is from Stanford and his PhD from the University of Washington.

Joan Steitz is HHMI Investigator and Henry Ford II Professor of Molecular Biophysics and Biochemistry at Yale University School of Medicine. Her research concerns the structure and function of small nuclear ribonucleoproteins. She is a member of the National Academy of Sciences and the American Academy of Arts and Sciences, and has received the National Medal of Science, the Warren Triennial Prize, and the Christopher Columbus Discovery Award in Biomedical Research, among many others. She teaches Principles of Biochemistry at Yale. Her bachelor's degree is from Antioch College and her PhD from Harvard University.

Charles Stevens is HHMI Investigator and Professor at The Salk Institute for Biological Studies and adjunct professor of pharmacology and neuroscience at the University of California at San Diego. His research focuses on the mechanisms of synaptic transmission. He taught at Yale University from 1975 until 1990. He is a member of the National Academy of Sciences and the American Academy of Arts and Sciences. He is on the steering committee for the NIH Alliance for Cellular Signaling. He received his bachelor's degree in psychology from Harvard University, MD from Yale University, and PhD in biophysics from Rockefeller University.

Samuel Ward is professor of molecular and cellular biology and professor of ecology and evolutionary biology at the University of Arizona. His research focuses on the genetic control of cellular morphogenesis during spermatogenesis in the nematode *C. elegans*, and genomic analysis of the germline. He directs the HHMI-funded undergraduate and precollege biology education program at the University of Arizona. He has been active with Project Kaleidoscope and chaired the NRC study committee that produced the report *The Role of Scientists in the Professional Development of Science Teachers.* His bachelor's degree is from Princeton University and his PhD is from California Institute of Technology.

C

Membership of the Panels and Workshop*

Bio2010 Chemistry Panel Roster

Ronald Breslow, Panel Leader, Columbia University
Arthur Ellis, University of Wisconsin-Madison
Marc Loudon, Purdue University
Jerry Mohrig, Carleton College
Jeanne Pemberton, University of Arizona
Dale Poulter, University of Utah
Sheldon Wettack, Harvey Mudd College

Bio2010 Physics and Engineering Panel Roster

John Hopfield, Panel Leader, Princeton University
Daniel Axelrod, University of Michigan
Scott Fraser, California Institute of Technology
Jonathon Howard, Max Planck Institute of Molecular Cell Biology and
    Genetics
Mimi Koehl, University of California-Berkeley
Carl Luchies, University of Kansas-Lawrence
Jose Onuchic, University of California-San Diego
Viola Vogel, University of Washington

---

*Biographical information is included in each summary.

Bio2010 Mathematics and Computer Science Panel Roster

Nancy Kopell, Panel Leader, Boston University
Robert Blystone, Trinity University
Louis J. Gross, University of Tennessee
Richard Karp, University of California-Berkeley
Eric Lander, Massachusetts Institute of Technology
Markus Meister, Harvard University
Alan Perelson, Los Alamos National Laboratory
Charles Peskin, New York University
Louise Ryan, Harvard University
Dewitt Sumners, Florida State University

Workshop Participants

Julian Adams, University of Michigan
Ann Burgess, University of Wisconsin-Madison
Malcolm Campbell, Davidson College
Denice Denton, University of Washington
Mike Doyle, Research Corporation
Billy Joe Evans, University of Michigan
Louis Gross, University of Tennessee
Keith Howard, Morehouse College
John Jungck, Beloit College
Priscilla Laws, Dickinson College
Jerry Mohrig, Carleton College
Jeanne Narum, Project Kaleidoscope
Fred Rudolph, Rice University
Patricia Soochan, Howard Hughes Medical Institute
Sheldon Wettack, Harvey Mudd College
Terry Woodin, National Science Foundation

SUMMARIES OF THE PANEL REPORTS

The committee would like to thank the members of the panels for their contribution to the report. The full texts of the panel reports presented to the committee are available from the Public Access Records Office at the National Research Council. Many of the ideas of the panels have been incorporated into the report, and other aspects of the panel reports influenced the committee's deliberations. Summaries of the panel reports are presented here to give the reader a sense of the full range of topics discussed by the panels.

D

Chemistry Panel Summary

The Chemistry panel met at the National Academy of Sciences building on February 15-16, 2001. They discussed the similarities and differences between undergraduate educations in biology versus chemistry. The following report includes examples of several initiatives in chemistry designed to improve undergraduate education.

EXPERTISE OF MEMBERS OF THE PANEL

Ronald Breslow is a University Professor and professor of chemistry and professor of biology at Columbia University. His research in bioorganic and physical organic chemistry includes the development of novel molecules and artificial enzymes. He is a former president of the American Chemical Society and was named "one of the top 75 contributors to the chemical enterprise in the past 75 years" by a 1997 poll conducted by Chemical and Engineering News. Among his many honors are the National Medal of Science and the Priestley Medal. He holds membership in the National Academy of Sciences, the American Philosophical Society, the American Academy of Arts and Sciences, the Royal Society of Great Britain and the Royal Society of Chemistry of London, as well as honorary membership in the Indian Academy of Sciences and the Japanese Chemical Society. He received the Columbia University Great Teacher Award and the Mark van Doren Medal for teaching, also awarded by Columbia University. His major research interest is currently the preparation of artificial enzymes that can imitate the function of natural enzymes. His graduate students typically design a potential catalyst on the computer, synthesize it, and then determine its catalytic effectiveness and the mechanism involved. His lab also synthesizes molecules that mimic antibodies or biological receptor sites; they construct molecules that will bind to polypeptides with sequence selectivity in water, using mainly hydrophobic interactions. He has bachelor's and PhD degrees in chemistry from Harvard University as well as a master's in medical science, also from Harvard.

Arthur Ellis is Meloche-Bascom Professor of Chemistry at the University of Wisconsin at Madison. His research program focuses on materials chemistry, including the use of the photoluminescence of semiconductors to develop new classes of chemical sensors. He received the American Chemical Society's George C. Pimentel Award in Chemical Education in 1997 and the Guggenheim Fellowship in 1989. He is the co-developer of modern instructional materials based on cutting-edge research, including texts, kits, demonstrations, and laboratory experiments. He also co-developed the Web site Innovations in SMET Education for the National Institute for Science Education. He co-organized a National Science Foundation workshop on the impact of technology on undergraduate mathematics and physical sciences. He served on the NRC Committee on Undergraduate Science Education from 1998 to 2000. He teaches chemistry at UW-Madison at the introductory, advanced undergraduate, and graduate level. He has a bachelor's degree from California Institute of Technology and a PhD from Massachusetts Institute of Technology, both in chemistry.

Marc Loudon is Gustav E. Cwalina Distinguished Professor of Medicinal Chemistry and associate dean for research and graduate programs in the School of Pharmacy and Pharmaceutical Sciences at Purdue University. He specializes in teaching organic chemistry to prepharmacy students and in developing group-study techniques for the course. His research interests are in the area of bioorganic chemistry, with specific interests in the HIV protease, carboxy-terminal peptide degradation, and peptide synthesis. In 2000, Loudon was named Indiana Professor of the Year by the Carnegie Foundation for the Advancement of Teaching. In 1999 he received the Charles B. Murphy Award, the Purdue University-wide teaching award. He was twice selected for the Henry Heine Award for Outstanding Teacher in Purdue's pharmacy school. Before coming to Purdue, he received the

Clark Teaching Prize from Cornell University's College of Arts and Sciences. He was also awarded Purdue's Helping Students Learn Award for developing innovative teaching techniques and has been instrumental in promoting undergraduate research programs in the pharmacy school. He is the author of *Organic Chemistry*, 3rd edition (Benjamin/Cummings) and study guides and animations on compact disk that accompany that text. The 4th edition of *Organic Chemistry* is under development and will be published by Oxford University Press. He is on the faculty of The Chemistry Place, a Web chemistry instructional project developed by Peregrine Publishers, Inc., and now owned by Addison-Wesley. He also served as co-chair of the committee that developed the Purdue University Teaching Evaluation System that is now being implemented. His current interests are in university administration, teaching, and the development of instructional materials. He is also co-editor, with Ken Houk of UCLA, of the Organic Chemistry Monograph Series of Oxford University Press. In collaboration with George Bodner in the Division of Chemical Education at Purdue, he has been developing a group-study approach to teaching organic chemistry, which has been implemented in the past several years in organic chemistry courses at Purdue. His research interests are in the area of bioorganic chemistry, with specific interests in the HIV protease, carboxy-terminal peptide degradation, and peptide synthesis. He received a bachelor's degree in chemistry from Louisiana State University and a PhD in physical-organic chemistry from University of California at Berkeley.

Jerry Mohrig is Herman and Gertrude Mosier Stark Professor in the Natural Sciences and professor of the natural sciences at Carleton College. His research is on the stereochemistry of base-catalyzed, addition-elimination reactions involving conjugated carbonyl compounds and the nature of biochemical catalysis by enzymes, its spatial characteristics, and evolution. Research in his group includes the stereochemistry of base-catalyzed, addition-elimination reactions involving conjugated carbonyl compounds among other topics, and over the past 25 years, it has involved over 130 undergraduate colleagues. He is the recipient of the 1989 James Flack Norris Award for Outstanding Achievement in the Teaching of Chemistry, given each year by the Northeastern Section of the American Chemical Society, and the Catalyst Award for Excellence in the Teaching of Chemistry (1978), from the Chemical Manufacturers Association. From 1989 to 1996, he served on the leadership committee for Project Kaleidoscope. He was a member of the NRC Advisory Board for the Center for Science,

Mathematics, and Engineering Education from 1995 to 1998. He is a member of the executive committee and the Molecular Basis of Life working group of the ChemLinks Coalition, an NSF-funded curriculum development project in undergraduate chemical education. He served as chair, treasurer, and president of the Council on Undergraduate Research. He was the chairman of the education and human resources committee of the Midwestern Association of Chemistry Teachers in Liberal Arts Colleges. He teaches introductory, organic, and bioorganic chemistry. He received a BS in chemistry from the University of Michigan and a PhD in chemistry from the University of Colorado.

Jeanne Pemberton is a professor of chemistry at the University of Arizona. Her research examines processes occurring at the surfaces of solids and the interfacial regions between phases. Specific interfacial systems of interest include electrochemical battery and electroluminescent and electrochromic devices; organized molecular assemblies at solid surfaces or air-water interfaces; chromatography stationary phase systems; soil and mineral systems important in the fate and transport of environmentally important chemicals; and surfaces such as ice, mineral acids, and alkali halides important in atmospheric processes. In 1990 and 1998, she received an award for special creativity from the National Science Foundation. She has also received the University of Arizona College of Science Distinguished Teaching Award and Faculty of Science Innovation in Teaching Award. She has served on the American Chemical Society's Committee on Professional Training and the NRC's Board on Chemical Sciences and Technology. For the National Science Foundation she has participated in a workshop on curricular reform in the analytical sciences and a review panel on course and curriculum reform/undergraduate faculty enhancement. She was a workshop leader for a Project Kaleidoscope session on "Making Connections: Is Chemistry the Central Science?" and served on a Department of Energy review panel on genome instrumentation research. She has a BS in chemistry and a BA in biology from the University of Delaware. Her PhD in chemistry is from the University of North Carolina at Chapel Hill.

Dale Poulter holds the John A. Widtsoe Distinguished Chair in the Department of Chemistry at the University of Utah. His research group works on problems at the interface between organic chemistry and biochemistry, including the mechanisms of the enzyme-catalyzed transformations and how the enzymes promote the reactions of the isoprene biosynthetic pathway. He also works on structure-function relationships in nucleic acids, in particular the topologies of complex naturally occurring RNAs, how their shapes relate to biological function, and what governs their interactions with other biopolymers during protein biosynthesis. His research group is interested in problems at the interface between organic chemistry and biochemistry. A major focus is the reactions catalyzed by enzymes in the isoprene biosynthetic pathway with special emphasis on establishing the mechanisms of the enzyme-catalyzed transformations and how the enzymes promote the reactions. Another area of interest is structure-function relationships in nucleic acids, in particular the topologies of complex naturally occurring RNAs, how their shapes relate to biological function and what governs their interactions with other biopolymers during protein biosynthesis. He was awarded the C. Cope Scholar Award of the American Chemical Society and serves on the ACS Committee on Professional Training. He is a Fellow of the American Association for the Advancement of Science. He received a bachelor's degree from Louisiana State University and a PhD from the University of California at Berkeley.

Sheldon Wettack is vice president and dean of faculty and professor of chemistry at Harvey Mudd College. He also attended the Institute for Educational Management at Harvard University. His initial academic appointment was in the chemistry department at Hope College, where he mentored about 30 undergraduates with support from a variety of individual research grants, including a Dreyfus Teacher-Scholar Award. His administrative work began when he was appointed dean for the natural sciences at Hope. He has served at the University of Richmond as arts and sciences dean and as president of Wabash College. He moved to Harvey Mudd in 1993. He is currently the project director of Harvey Mudd's NSF-AIRE grant and of the Claremont Colleges' technology grant from the Mellon Foundation. He has an AB and MA from San Jose State College and a PhD in physical chemistry from University of Texas-Austin.

REPORT OF THE CHEMISTRY PANEL

Much of modern biology has become increasingly chemical in character. This has always been true of biochemistry and medicinal chemistry, but molecular biology, genetics, cell biology, proteomics, physiology, microbiology, neurobiology, agriculture, and many other divisions of biology are now using chemistry as a major part of their language and their research. The trend will continue, as more and more biological phenomena are explained in fundamental chemical terms. Many biology departments recognize this reality and trend and require significant numbers of chemistry courses for their majors. The panel recommended that all future biological research students have an effective working knowledge of concepts and skills in chemistry (as listed in Chapter 2 of the committee report). In order to achieve such knowledge, formal courses are needed. Students who are planning on careers in biological research should take at least two years of chemistry courses taught in chemistry departments. Furthermore, even those biology students whose career goals are unsure should take such a program. It will be important and is normally required for medical students; those in allied fields such as nursing, or in biology-based fields such as agriculture, will be well served by having a basic understanding of chemistry. Their education is preparing them for careers in which, over the next 40 years, those without a basic grounding in chemistry will be increasingly lost. Some biology teachers may feel uncomfortable requiring students to learn more chemistry than they themselves understand or use, but this attitude is a disservice to the students. The future is different from the present, and students just undertaking scientific careers need a basic education different from that of 20 years ago, when the sciences were not all so integrated.

Students need their chemistry background as soon as possible, so that their biology courses containing biochemistry and other chemistry-based material can be taught on a sophisticated level. In particular, the attempts in some biology departments to teach biochemistry without requiring students to have a knowledge of organic chemistry turns the course into a baffling exercise in acronyms, not chemical structures. The panel felt that whenever possible biology students should take the needed chemistry course sequence continuously starting in their freshman year. Currently, many chemistry departments teach a full year of general chemistry and then follow it with a full year of organic chemistry. However, there are alternatives. In some institutions, the first-year course is organic chemistry, followed by a general chemistry course in the second year. One of the most interesting plans is at Barnard College. There, the first semester is a general chemistry course, and the organic chemistry sequence starts in the second semester. The second semester of organic chemistry comes in the fall of the second year, and that spring the students can take a course in physical chemistry. The revised sequence has a number of advantages. Students who are taking only one year of chemistry can be exposed to both the concepts and content of general chemistry and some organic chemistry. Furthermore, it would be possible to teach the one-semester organic course as an introduction, covering all the major classes of compounds and reactions in an introductory way. Then the second semester of organic chemistry could be more intensive, introducing ideas of mechanism and of biological relevance. Since organic chemistry is really not a linear subject, there is some advantage in having the students know something about carbonyl chemistry, for instance, rather early rather than waiting until the second semester to teach it. This would give biology students a reasonable background for their second-year biology courses. The panel asked that chemistry departments consider a plan in which general chemistry is a one-semester course, followed by the first semester of organic chemistry in the spring of the first year. Then in the fall of the second year an additional semester of organic chemistry could be taught, with the opportunity in the spring for a course in analytical chemistry, in physical chemistry, or in some combination of the two.

Proposal for beginning chemistry curriculum (presented in semesters, used by 75 percent of schools)

Semester 1   Introductory

Semester 2   Organic Chemistry—Concepts

Semester 3   Organic Chemistry—Details, connections, biochemical examples, and including physical chemistry in solution and information on instruments for NMR, GC, etc.

Semester 4   Physical and Analytical Chemistry (including some topics removed from introductory course) and Biochemistry

The panel identified the following five issues that might hamper the changes it recommended:

• A drawback of making the introductory course only a one-semester course is a decreased opportunity to include interdisciplinary examples. In addition, poorly prepared students may be left further behind by a one-semester introductory course despite not needing the specific skills for organic chemistry.

• Many students do not take introductory chemistry until their second year and then take organic as juniors. (For example, at Carleton, two-thirds of the biology majors in organic chemistry are juniors.)

• Chemistry has some of the strictest prerequisite requirements. This pushes biochemistry late in the undergraduate career after students have already had many biology courses and they may miss the connections.

• Transfer students may be disadvantaged. At University of Wisconsin-Madison, 50 percent of chemistry majors are transfers from two-year schools, and they are the source of most of the demographic diversity in the department.

• This proposal would require the development of a new analytical/physical chemistry course. The University of Michigan tried and failed to do something similar. One challenge is to convince analytical and physical chemists that life science students are a good target audience for their teaching.

Connections Between Chemistry and Biology

In the United States, most students enrolled in the first two years of chemistry courses have at least an interest in biology, and many hope to follow careers in biology or medicine. This is quite different from the situation in Europe and Asia, in which chemistry courses are taught exclusively to chemistry majors. U.S. classes in the first two years of chemistry contain biology majors, premedical students, engineering students, environmental science students, and non-science students simply meeting a science requirement, in addition to prospective chemists. The need to educate future chemists does not mean that chemistry teachers should pay no attention to the needs and interests of biology students. The panel felt it was important for chemistry teachers to take into account the interests of all their students, and not pretend that they are all chemistry majors. In particular, when possible, the teachers should include biological examples to make it clear that the fundamental science being taught has clear implications for current biology. If possible, they should also indicate what is still left to be discovered in biology for which chemistry can supply answers. Of course, teachers should also refer to environmental examples, such as the relevance of free radical chain reactions to the ozone hole. Real-life examples are of interest to all students, so even the engineering students will find biological and environmental chemistry a stimulating part of a course. For that matter, biology students can find the contrast between laboratory chemistry and manufacturing processes interesting if the examples are well chosen. It does not seem practical to break chemistry courses up into different sections, addressed to different student interests. Furthermore, interests change—a biology student might well go into environmental studies, for instance. Thus the critical recommendation is that chemistry teachers not simply teach "pure" chemistry, but instead stimulate student interest by showing the breadth of the current science and future science in which chemistry has an important role to play.

Some students complain that much of what they are learning in chemistry courses does not seem to be directly relevant to their current interests. Such complaints often confuse the roles of education and of training. Training may well address the current needs of students—how to clone a protein, for instance. Education gives them the base on which to build understanding of future scientific advances. Such understanding is needed for them to function creatively in the science of the future, and it is also needed for their self-respect. Even if they could perform cloning by following a recipe, with no understanding of what is going on, this would reduce them to narrow technicians rather than competent scientists.

Many courses on organic chemistry are currently taught as sets of disconnected facts. Students would benefit from a combinatorial approach emphasizing principles and concepts. Organic chemistry students often have difficulty translating what they have learned with simple molecules into an understanding of macromolecular behavior. Complex processes should be covered in class. Some professors have experimented with teaching the topics of a traditional yearlong organic class in a new format. All topics are covered quickly during the first semester. This gives the students a general understanding of the concepts. It helps them to see how they are interconnected when each topic is repeated in greater detail during the second semester. The first semester is principle-oriented, not watered down. This approach also allows more biochemical topics to be introduced during the second semester. This twice-through approach is used in Dan Kim's book at MIT. Dale Poulter tried it with his classes at the University of Utah. He found the students to be very frustrated during the first four weeks of the first semester. However, by the end of that semester, the students were happy, and he was satisfied with what they had learned.

Example Course

In his organic chemistry course at Carleton College, Jerry Mohrig integrates material on carbohydrates (which he believes are undervalued by the chemistry community) by having a capstone to his yearlong course on "Why do we get the flu every year?" Information on glycobiology, molecular recognition, and cell-cell interactions is integrated throughout both semesters as a storyline. Originally, he had tried to use multiple isolated biological examples but the relevance wasn't clear to his students. The flu example was chosen instead of details on how egg and sperm bind because more is known about the viral system. (Ron Breslow noted that it is crucial to communicate to students that there are still open questions like these to be investigated.)

A noticeable change in students' attitudes was seen when biology professors later taught the same concepts previously covered in chemistry class. It appeared that by discussing what the students had learned in chemistry class, the biology faculty demonstrated how chemistry is essential to fully understand biological systems. These connections help students to make desirable interdisciplinary connections. Their understanding of the material was tested by asking students one or two years after learning about the flu example to answer a question on immunological aspects of influenza. The flu case will be published shortly by Wylie and it is being written up as part of a collection of modules suitable for organic chemistry by T. Andrew Mobley at Grinnell. It will also be described in the *Journal of Chemical Education*.

Laboratories

Chemistry courses normally have laboratory work, either as part of the course or separately. These labs have two functions: to teach students the skills they will need if they are to go on to experimental science related to chemistry, and to show students that what they have learned in lectures has a real-world aspect. However, these undergraduate labs are too often exercises in following a recipe, exercises that do not sufficiently excite and inspire students. This is a wasted opportunity. To give a better sense of what science is, and how research is done, the panel felt that when possible the elementary labs be project based, with groups of students cooperating to solve a problem, for instance, by collecting data or running a reaction under different conditions to try to optimize it. The students should also prepare reports of their studies and results. The panel generally wanted to counter the "tyranny of the one-week approach" to lab. Many ideas were presented on how to provide students with project-centered experiences. A related issue was the difficulty in balancing teaching of process and teaching of skills in labs. Problem-based learning can also help in that regard; Bio2010 committee member Sam Ward has a lot of experience with this.

He may have ideas on how we can create proposals that are scalable and portable so many students can benefit.

Harvey Mudd College (HMC) has many unique laboratory experiences. Seniors do independent laboratory research or computer science/ engineering clinics in which they work on real-world problems suggested by industry. All introductory biology labs are project-oriented. First-year students are offered a choice of traditional labs in chemistry and physics or an Interdisciplinary (ID) Lab that combines chemistry and physics. HMC has broad scientific core requirements as well as a colloquium program within each department. The college is also instituting new majors that cross disciplinary boundaries such as a joint math-biology major.

The ID Lab at HMC is a stand-alone course not affiliated with a lecture, although a large lab manual does provide background information. It creates excitement by presenting material in a more research-like setting. The students work in pairs for a three-week experiment before shifting partners for the next three weeks. The lab provides ownership by letting students decide which questions to ask. This can lead to increased interest on the part of the student when a related topic is presented in a later lecture course. It gives the opportunity to think like a scientist as well as across disciplines. The ID Lab was developed with an Award for the Integration of Research and Education (AIRE) from NSF. The goal of the ID Lab is to make the first year of college more exciting. HMC faculty spent a summer working with eight undergraduates to develop the course and get it ready for implementation. These labs do not cost much extra in materials (although laptop computers are useful); however, they do require extensive instructor time. In the ID Lab at HMC, there are three faculty for 36 students. Each student goes to one four-hour session per week. In the three-week experiment they spend week #1 on skills and equipment; at home they start designing the experiment to do during week #2. Week #3 provides time to finish up, analyze results, and present orally. A written report is also done. The grades are based on prelab write-ups, final reports, and lab behavior. The student evaluations indicated that they liked being able to think creatively and being immersed in the subject. Assessment was done by comparing answers to a question about paramecium and contractile vacuoles between students from the ID Lab and those in traditional chemistry and physics labs. An outside professor from Pomona College was brought in to score the assessment. The only areas of difference were in error analysis and development of creative proposals; the ID students performed better in both of these areas. Both groups understood the fundamentals.

Purdue has an integrated laboratory for 120 pharmacy students. The TAs come from multiple departments and the experiments range from patient consultations to analyses of receptor binding. In some experiments the students contribute questions and influence the course of the lab. To come together and do this, the departments required a mandate from the dean.

Many students now arrive in college with computer skills, and such skills can greatly enhance their educational experience in chemistry courses. The panel recommended that chemistry instructors think of ways to get students working independently or in groups on computers. Examples could include doing molecular modeling of the compounds and reactions being studied in lectures or labs, going into the chemical literature by computer to retrieve information and procedures, and perhaps even writing small programs to handle the information collected in project-based labs.

Teaching Materials

Not all chemistry teachers are aware of the relevant biological examples that could broaden the scope of their courses, and not all chemistry texts have such examples. The panel felt that the teaching of chemistry would be greatly facilitated by the production of materials that illustrate the interplay of chemistry and biology that could be used to supplement the textbooks. Some important topics are included in organic chemistry texts, usually at the back of the book. Teachers often do not get that far. For instance, the chemistry of heterocyclic compounds is often given short shrift at best in many elementary organic chemistry classes, and yet heterocycles are components of nucleic acids, vitamins, and proteins, and their chemistry is central to much of biochemistry. Almost all medicinal compounds contain heterocyclic components. As another example, phosphate esters are part of nucleic acids and coenzymes, but their chemistry is often neglected in elementary organic chemistry courses. The contrast in properties between carboxylic esters and phosphate esters has important basic chemistry lessons, but is usually neglected. The panel encouraged the teachers of elementary chemistry courses to think carefully about which topics they include and exclude, and not be tempted to teach only the most topical current chemistry research findings at the expense of covering basic and important material that they may personally find less exciting. Of course, every teacher wants to bring exciting topics into a course, and some material that illustrates the magic of chemistry itself is essential. However, chemistry claims to be the central, useful, and creative science, and its relevance to other fields will help justify this claim. Some non-chemistry students find chemistry particularly difficult; with some effort on the part of the chemistry faculty, they may conclude the difficulty is worth it.

Modules can help mitigate the risks faculty take in changing their courses. They provide supporting material to the instructor. Books as companions to traditional texts are useful. One companion is a materials chemistry supplement to traditional inorganic courses with illustrations of how to incorporate examples involving solids. The companion was produced by Art Ellis and colleagues at the Institute for Chemical Education of the University of Wisconsin. The companion provides a matrix indicating which examples fit with which chapters of traditional textbooks. In making the matrix, the authors decided that they needed to agree at "low resolution" on what concepts should be covered (stoichiometry, structure and binding, for example) but that a "high resolution" consensus was unnecessary because faculty members could choose their own examples from among those provided in order to illustrate the common big themes.

The National Institute for Science Education (NISE) at the University of Wisconsin-Madison was created by cooperative agreement with NSF. The goal of NISE is to enhance student experiences via teacher training. Evidence shows that collaborative learning leads to gains in performance, attitude, and persistence. NISE targets "reform ready" instructors to maximize gains. They gather stories of obstacles and results from colleagues and provide guidance on how to use interviews, portfolios, and scoring rubrics for assessment. In addition they focus on learning through technology across various disciplines and institutions. Some of the instructional material includes a DNA Optical Transform Kit, magnets, and ferrofluids. These materials are provided at-cost by the Institute for Chemical Education.

The NSF ChemLinks project is a systemic change initiative that focuses on the role of chemistry as a filter for other scientific disciplines. It is run by Brock Spencer at Beloit College and is associated with a Berkeley consortium. It provides two to three week teaching modules and a book of these modules was published by Wylie. The only one related to biology is called "Would you like fries with that? What is all the fuss about fat in the diet?"

A 1998 NSF report *Curricular Developments in the Analytical Sciences,* is available from its committee chair, Ted Kuwana at the University of Kansas. (*http://www.chem.ukans.edu/tkuwana/*). The committee was formed in response to a perceived failure of the curriculum to meet the needs of scientists, especially industrial employers looking for employees with quantitative skills, trained in measurement science, and with more real-world, problem analysis skills. Three crucial areas that students lack are measurement, problem solving, and hands-on techniques. One way to improve these areas is to use context-based material and problem-based learning (PBL). Through PBL, students are taught to: (1) define a problem, (2) deal with sampling, (3) separate out interfering compounds, (4) measure, (5) collect data, and (6) analyze results. All science students need to know about analysis, instruments, and quantitative concepts. For example, biology students need to know which columns to choose for which experiments. Biologists also need to learn about spectroscopy, especially NMR and mass spectroscopy, but not necessarily infrared spectroscopy. They need to acquire analytical and problem-solving skills and have exposure to primary experimental data. In the context of chemistry, the best way to teach these topics is through an analytical course.

Panel member Art Ellis mentioned the book "Talking About Leaving." Ellis has eliminated grading on the curve and, therefore, much of the competition in his introductory course. He uses exercises to make the students feel less isolated, including study groups and ConcepTests. In this approach, conceptual questions are posed in the lecture room along with a few possible answers. Students vote on the possible answers, try to persuade their neighbors in the lecture room that they are correct, and finally vote again. The goal is to get students to predict how things work; it requires inspiration, not more acid-base calculations. This form of peer instruction is often an effective pedagogical method, and it also provides the instructor with online feedback as to how well the class is following the lecture. It can also help to decrease differences between students of diverse backgrounds. Ellis recommends using good, pointed questions to focus the material. He focuses on having students spend time in discussion groups and he covers the key points in lecture, but requires them to read the textbook for the remainder of the content. He views this as empowering them to learn. Tracking at UW-Madison shows that enrollment for organic chemistry is almost as large as introductory chemistry; therefore attrition has declined with these new efforts in the first-year course.

Implementation

Marc Loudon summarized his impressions of the panel's discussions. Real-world examples are necessary for chemistry courses (like Jerry Mohrig's flu stories), analytical tools are crucial, and teaching methods must excite the students (like HMC's ID Lab and Art Ellis' materials). How to transfer some of the techniques to large schools is a real issue.

In order to successfully implement change, crucial skills and themes must be identified so that tests measure learning of important material. Other obstacles will also be encountered. Many schools find it hard to optimally allocate resources, and there are big drawbacks to basing money on the number of student hours. In addition, the assigning of TAs is important. Do biology or chemistry graduate students act as TAs in biochemistry courses? The choice dramatically affects how the students see the material. A workshop could be organized to bring together faculty and administrators to discuss the importance of these structural issues. Project Kaleidoscope is one venue that attempts to address such problems. It operates by looking for "what works" and encouraging others to apply those approaches in their own institutions, departments, and courses. It has recently focused on two main issues in educational reform: the importance of institutional change and the architectural design of laboratories and classrooms. In addition, its network of Faculty for the 21st Century provides support for young professors who care about education by linking them with similar faculty at other institutions.

The American Chemical Society (ACS) Committee on Professional Training (CPT) oversees undergraduate accreditation in chemistry at over 600 schools. Their 40-page guidelines are available at the CPT Web site (*http://www.acs.org/education/cpt/guidelines.html*). The guidelines describe a chemistry curriculum at the core level and provide topical supplements in areas such as biochemistry. Biochemistry was recently added as a requirement for all chemistry majors. There are three ways a school can satisfy that requirement for accreditation: a core required course, an upper-level course, or distribution of biochemical content throughout the core curriculum. The third option would go a long way toward helping to address the perceived irrelevance of chemistry to biologists. However, most schools will stick with a separate biochemistry course. One reason for this concern is the fear of classically trained chemistry faculty who themselves lack biological training and do not have easy access to good textbooks with integrated biological examples.

The trend of the ACS's CPT is to allow for increased flexibility in how departments meet requirements. They see the flexibility as a necessary response to today's chemistry, which is more broad-based than in the past. ACS is focusing on providing more options for individual students and for institutions while maintaining the same level of rigor and expertise. Flexibility can be hampered by faculty who act as if they are slaves to textbooks. To provide the options discussed here will require new formats of textbooks. For example, Marc Loudon mentioned the new option of ordering certain chapters of a larger book directly from the publisher, who will assemble a packet specifically for a course. This allows professors to choose the modules they want. Ron Breslow pointed out that this is easier for general chemistry than for organic.

Most sciences have a national organization that deals with many special concerns of the field. Biology is in an unusual position—the various divisions of biology have their own national organizations, and only the Federation of American Societies for Experimental Biology (FASEB) speaks for all. But FASEB does not perform many of the central functions that are common for national organizations in other sciences. For example, the American Chemical Society's Committee on Professional Training is concerned with examining and improving the education and training received by undergraduate and graduate students in chemistry. FASEB has no such committee.

Because biology has no committee on professional education and training, the Bio2010 Committee has been formed on a one-time basis to address biology education, including the amount and type of chemistry education that biology students need. The current ad hoc committee is not an adequate substitute for a continuing body with the responsibility to monitor and recommend the content of education programs for biology students. Thus, the panel saw a need for FASEB to become a more substantial national body, and, in particular, that it form a Committee on Education and Training to function on a continuing basis, as the American Chemical Society Committee on Professional Training does in chemistry.

CHEMISTRY CONCEPTS AND SKILLS POSED AS QUESTIONS

The Periodic Table

Concepts
a. What are the trends going horizontally?
b. What are the trends going vertically?

e.g., why is H_2O different from H_2S in acidity? in boiling point? in reactivity toward oxidizing agents?

e.g., why are thioesters less stabilized by resonance than are oxygen esters? how does this affect their biochemical properties?

e.g., why are biological molecules based on carbon, not silicon or germanium?

e.g., why is iron used as an oxidant in enzymes, while zinc is not?

e.g., what is electronegativity, and how does it vary going horizontally and vertically?

Skills

Students should be able to:

a. write the electronic configurations of the elements in the first two horizontal rows, including the atomic orbitals involved

b. reproduce the first two rows of the periodic table from memory, so they do not have to look it up constantly

c. specify which are the metals, which are not

Atoms

Concepts

a. What are the shapes of 1s, 2s, and 2p orbitals? Of 3d orbitals?

b. What are the shapes and angles of hybrid orbitals? How are they constructed from simple atomic orbitals?

c. Why do the electrons in an atom not simply fall into the nucleus?

d. Why do atoms absorb light at only certain frequencies (or wavelengths)?

Properties of Molecules

Concepts

a. What is the basis of covalent bonding?

b. What are sigma bonds? Pi bonds?

c. What is a bond energy?

d. What are the approximate bond energies of a C-H bond? A C-C single bond? a C=C double bond?

e. Which molecules can exist as cis/trans (Z/E) isomers?

f. Which molecules can exist as enantiomers? As diastereomers?

g. Which molecules will have dipole moments, and why?

h. Why does ethanol dissolve in water, while diethyl ether does not?

i. What factors determine the boiling points of compounds?

j. What factors determine the acidity or basicity of a molecule? What are the approximate pK's of carboxylic acids such as acetic acid, and of amines such as triethylamine?

k. At pH 7, what is the state of ionization of glycine, of lysine, of glutamic acid, in water?

l. What is an ion pair? What is a hydrogen bond? What is the hydrophobic effect? What is the role of van der Waals forces in molecular association?

m. What is pyridine? imidazole? pyrimidine? phenol? folic acid? thiamine? pyridoxal? NAD? NADP?

n. What is the structure of ATP? of coenzyme A? of heme?

o. What is the structure of liquid water?

Skills

Students should be able to:

a. Predict the three-dimensional structure of a molecule from its two-dimensional representation.

b. Specify the axial and equatorial conformations of substituents in cyclic compounds such as steroids and carbohydrates.

c. Write the structures of the building blocks of common biomolecules, such as the amino acids, the nucleotides, and the simple fatty acids and carbohydrates.

d. Classify the sidechains of the amino acids as polar and non-polar, and indicate what relevance this has to the structure of proteins in water.

e. Write the two-dimensional structure of a molecule from its chemical name.

f. Look at a picture of a molecular model of a protein and understand what it represents.

g. Write resonance structures for various delocalized molecules.

Properties of Macromolecules and Materials

Concepts

a. What are the covalent linkages in proteins, nucleic acids, and polysaccharides?

b. What factors determine the three-dimensional conformational structures of these biopolymers?

c. What happens when a protein is denatured?

d. What are the structures of micelles? Of biological membranes?

e. How can one measure the size of a protein?

f. What is an ultracentrifuge?

g. What makes a metal a good electrical conductor? What is a semiconductor?

Reactions

Concepts

a. What are the principal reaction types in organic chemistry?

b. What are biochemical examples of these reaction types?

c. What are the reactive intermediates in some of these types, such as carbocations and carbanions, free radicals, enols and enolates?

d. What are the detailed mechanisms by which such typical reactions occur?

e. What is a transition state for a reaction, sometimes called the activated complex?

f. What determines the value of the equilibrium constant in a chemical reaction? What is the role of enthalpy, entropy, and free energy? What is entropy?

g. What is pH? What is a pK? What is a buffer?

h. What determines the rate of a chemical reaction? How does it depend on the concentrations of the reactants? What is the meaning of kinetic order? What is the effect of temperature?

i. What is a catalyst for a reaction? How do enzymes catalyze biochemical reactions?

j. What is the Principle of Microscopic Reversibility? How is the acceleration of a reaction achieved by a catalyst related to the acceleration of the reverse reaction? How are the catalytic mechanisms of the forward and reverse reactions related?

k. What is the Steady State Approximation?

l. What is the Michaelis-Menten equation for enzyme-catalyzed reactions?

m. What does it mean if a reaction rate is said to be diffusion limited?

n. What is the relationship between the concentration of a substance and its activity? What is an activity coefficient?

o. How is it possible for the rate of bromination of acetone to have no dependence on the concentration of bromine, provided that concentration is above a certain level?

p. What is an oxidation potential? How is it related to the free energy change for electron transfer reactions?

q. What is the meaning of the half-life in radioactive decay?

Skills

Students should be able to:

a. calculate the buffer ratio needed to achieve a given pH from the pKa of the buffer components.

b. write the kinetic expressions corresponding to various simple reaction mechanisms, including the correct time and concentration dimensions.

c. analyze whether an enzyme inhibitor is competitive or non-competitive from the kinetic plot.

d. explain what competitive and non-competitive inhibition indicates about the likely mechanism of inhibition.

e. write a balanced equation for an oxidation reaction, for instance.

Analytical and Spectroscopic Measurements

Concepts

a. what physical process is involved in the absorption of ultraviolet light? of infrared light?

b. what process is involved in the diffraction of x-rays?

c. what is electrophoresis?

d. what is HPLC? gas chromatography? mass spectrometry?

e. what is fluorescence? phosphorescence?

f. what does ESR measure?

g. what is the physical process involved in nuclear magnetic resonance?

h. what determines the chemical shift of a proton in NMR? its coupling constant with another proton?

i. which common nuclei can be detected by NMR?

Skills

Students should be able to:

a. examine an NMR spectrum and indicate the chemical shifts and coupling constants for the various signals.

b. predict the NMR spectrum that would be seen for the protons of ethanol, and for the carbons of ethanol.

E

Physics and Engineering Panel Summary

The panel on physics and engineering met on February 25-26, 2001, at the National Academy of Sciences building. The panel devoted most of its effort to the discussion of appropriate content for an introductory physics course. They also considered the role of engineering in the study of biology and ways to help students understand the concept of systems that is so crucial to engineering, and becoming more central to biomedical research.

EXPERTISE OF MEMBERS OF THE PANEL

John Hopfield is Howard A. Prior Professor in the Life Sciences and Professor of Molecular Biology at Princeton University. His research encompasses neurobiology and computing networks. He is a member of the National Academy of Sciences, the American Academy of Arts and Sciences, and the American Philosophical Society. He has received the MacArthur Fellowship and the APS prize in Biophysics and was named California Scientist of the Year for 1991. He has taught in physics departments (from first-year physics to graduate condensed matter physics), in chemistry departments (first-year chemistry to graduate biophysical chemistry), and now in a molecular biology department, where he teaches a senior course related to how networks of neuron-like elements compute. He has a bachelor's degree from Swarthmore College and PhD from Cornell.

Daniel Axelrod is a professor of physics at the University of Michigan. His research is on the development of optical microscopy techniques to study dynamics at biological surfaces and membranes. He has taught extensively, including courses on Physics and Music, Biophysical Principles of Microscopy, Techniques in Molecular Biophysics, Dynamics of Biophysical Processes, Science and Strategy in the Nuclear Arms Race, Living with Physics, and Introductory Modern Physics. He is a Fellow of the Biophysical Society and has received the Excellence in Teaching Award from the University of Michigan. He has a bachelor's degree in physics and math from Brooklyn College and a PhD in physics from the University of California at Berkeley.

Scott Fraser is the co-director of the Center for Computational Molecular Biology and Anna L. Rosen Professor of Biology at California Institute of Technology. His research explores the mechanisms involved in the assembly of the vertebrate nervous system, in particular, the patterning of cell lineages, cell migration, and axonal connections. He is involved in developing new imaging technologies (modification of optics of light microscopes, new software for acquisition, and manipulation of data) at the Biological Imaging Center of the Beckman Institute with a goal of developing methods to observe single cells in intact developing embryos. He is the recipient of the Marcus Singer Medal and the McKnight Scholar Award and is a fellow of the American Academy of Arts and Sciences. He received the Kaiser-Permanente Award for Best Medical School Teaching and the Silver Beaker Award for Best Medical School Faculty Member. Among the many courses he has taught at Caltech are Principles of Modern Microscopy, Fundamentals of Modern Biology, and Developmental Neurobiology. In addition he has taught summer courses at Cold Spring Harbor. He received his bachelor's degree from Harvey Mudd College and his PhD from Johns Hopkins University.

Jonathon Howard is a professor of physiology and biophysics at the University of Washington. He was recently named a director at the Max Planck Institute for Molecular Cell Biology and Genetics. His research is on the mechanical properties of cells and molecules focusing on the motor protein kinesin. He was a PEW Scholar in 1990 and was awarded a Guggenheim Fellowship in 1996. He has a bachelor's degree in pure mathematics and a PhD in neurobiology, both from Australian National University.

Mimi Koehl is a professor in the Integrative Biology Department at the University of California at Berkeley. Her research involves the application of fluid dynamics and solid mechanics to study how biological structures function in nature. She utilizes this approach to investigate the various ways in which organisms withstand and utilize the movement of water or air around them. She has been awarded the Presidential Young Investigator Award and two achievement awards from Gettysburg College. She has received NATO, Guggenheim, and MacArthur fellowships. Her teaching experience includes Animal Biology, Physiology, Biomechanics and Structure, The Mechanics of Organisms, The Biology of Rocky Seashores, and Living Machines. She is on the scientific advisory board for *The Shape of Life*, a National Geographic television series about animal form, function, and evolution. She was elected as a member of the National Academy of Sciences in 2001. She received her bachelor's degree from Gettysburg College in Pennsylvania and her PhD in zoology from Duke University.

Carl Luchies is a professor of mechanical engineering at the University of Kansas at Lawrence. He is also the director of the Human Performance Laboratory, located in the Center on Aging, University of Kansas Medical Center. His research is on biomechanics including human balance and mobility. He previously taught at Hope College in Holland, Michigan, where he developed a liberal-arts-based engineering education program. He has taught courses in computer-aided design, statics, solid mechanics, material science, vibrations, thermodynamics, and fluid mechanics. He received his bachelor's degree from Calvin College and PhD from the University of Michigan.

Jose Onuchic is a professor of physics at the University of California at San Diego. His research in theoretical biophysics and chemical physics focuses on theory of chemical reactions in condensed matter and rational design of functional proteins. He is a member of the Molecular Biophysics Training Grant Steering Committee at UCSD and served on UCSD's Task Force on Biological Sciences. He was awarded the Engineering Institute Prize, Sao Paulo, Brazil, in 1980 and the International Centre for Theoretical Physics Prize in Honor of Professor Werner Heisenberg, Trieste, Italy, in 1988. He was named an associate member of the Academia de Ciencias do Estado de Sao Paulo, a Beckman Young Investigator, a Fellow of the American Physical Society, and a Senior Fellow of SDSC, a national laboratory for computational science and engineering. He is part of a team recently awarded a biocomplexity grant from NSF. He received his bachelor's degrees in electrical engineering and physics from Universidade de Sao Paulo in Brazil and his PhD from California Institute of Technology

Viola Vogel is director of the Center for Nanotechnology and professor of bioengineering at the University of Washington. Her research program is focused on investigating how to control the assembly of molecular building blocks into supramolecular complexes with predictable architecture. It involves nanoscale surface patterning, molecular motors and switches, biomaterials, assembly of extracellular matrix proteins, cell/surface interactions, biomineralization, surface analysis, optical spectroscopy, and microscopy. She received her PhD in physics from Johann-Wolfgang Goethe University in Frankfurt/Main

REPORT OF THE PHYSICS AND ENGINEERING PANEL

The panel devoted most of its effort to the discussion of appropriate content for an introductory physics course. The concepts that they felt were appropriate are listed in the body of the report. The panel concluded that physics plays three roles in the education of the future research biologist. First, there are the specific and quantitative principles of physics on which a microscopic understanding of biology is ultimately based, and on which much of the instrumentation of biological research is also based. Understanding better how these principles are reflected in biology becomes important as biological research becomes more quantitative, develops further quantitative models, and becomes even more heavily reliant on experimental physical techniques. Second, and more abstract, physics is a more mature science with far less complexity than biology, in which a student can more easily learn about the interactive relationship between experiments, theory, modeling, and analysis. Third, much of physics is about the behavior of dynamical systems. Biologists need to understand dynamics, for biology is fundamentally a driven, dissipative system, not an equilibrium system. For most students, 1 to 1.5 years of a physics course *with an appropriate curriculum* can make significant progress toward accomplishing these three objectives. Additional physics-based and engineering-based courses emphasizing biology should also be available at major institutions. The panel anticipates that an increasing number of physics/engineering majors or double majors in physics/engineering and biology will go into graduate education in biology.

The panel listed three questions that might be asked about the content of an introductory physics course: What background is needed? How can that background material be structured into a course? What other material needs to be added in order to make the course understandable? An appropriate yearlong course of more or less conventional format but revised content is described in the main text of the report. Given the increased emphasis of that course on physical measurement techniques, dynamical systems, modeling, and quantitative analysis, the panel felt that it was appropriate to address the question of balance between chemistry, physics, engineering, mathematics, and computer science in the new curriculum. In view of the importance for biology of materials that cannot be addressed within a one-year physics course, offering an optional additional physics course is strongly recommended by the panel. Ideas for this course are outlined below. The panel felt that the biologists of 2010—on the average—would be better served by these additions to the physics curriculum than an *obligatory* third quarter (or second semester) of organic chemistry.

Potential Additions to the Physics Concepts Described in the Body of the Report

The physics concepts listed in the body of the report could potentially fit into a yearlong introductory course. However, the panel felt that additional concepts of physics would also be useful to biology students. The following list indicates those topics they recommend adding to the curriculum in schools where biology students are able to take a four-quarter or three-semester sequence of physics. Some of these topics might also be substituted for concepts in the list found in the body of the report, depending on the interests of the students or the instructor.

- Particle in a box; energy levels; spectroscopy from a quantum viewpoint
- Representation of optical spectra as a distribution of oscillators absorbing and emitting energy
- Forster Transfer; quenching; photon-counting noise/statistics
- Other microscopies: electron, scanning tunneling, atomic force
- Networks – Neural/chemical/genetic (This goes well with electrical circuit analysis—should also do a laboratory with real circuits. This area connects well to biological examples.)
- Spontaneous static pattern formation and symmetry breaking (mag-

netization—from microscopics to the magnetic phase transition; the liq-
uid-gas interface; handedness of quartz crystals
   • Spontaneous dynamical pattern formation (wind-driven surface
waves in water, stripe formation in sedimentation, circulation patterns in
water heated from below, the BZ reaction, slime mold aggregation)
   • Chaos and periodicity; chaotic systems in physics (coupled oscillators, onset of turbulence) and in biology (population dynamics, heartbeat)
   • Electromagnetism and magnetic properties of matter: B, H, dipole
fields, forces on magnetized particles, how fMRI originates from magnetic
properties of hemoglobin; magnetic bacteria and nerve cells.

   The panel envisions the teaching of a one-year course derived from the
physics concepts in the body of the report. Some portions of such an
introductory physics course could be relatively conventional. The course
might well begin with classical mechanics (because it is the basis for a kinetic understanding of chemistry). Gravity would be included—not because it is historic and conventional (which it is) but because it is an excellent pedagogical subject for understanding mechanics. The course might
initially treat heat in the usual fashion as the "byproduct" of dissipative
forces and explore the second law of thermodynamics from the conventional 19th-century viewpoint. However, added to the chosen subset of
topics from today's introductory physics is a focus on the parts of physics
relevant to biology at the molecular level, and on aspects of macrocsopic
physics relevant to biological functions. A totally different pedagogy, of
more relevance to molecular biology, beginning at the microscopic level,
might be developed as an alternative course of study. The level of the
course would depend to some degree on the amount of material students
have already learned in their high school science courses.
   The existence of superb simulation tools for visualizing the predictions
of a set of physics equations should be strongly used in homework problem
sets. These tools free the student from the tyranny of only considering the
limited "special problems" that are exactly solvable, allow the student to
experiment beyond their ability to carry out the manipulations of classical
mathematics, are wonderful tools any time statistical ideas are a part of the
physics, and, in addition, are now important tools for any scientist. These
tools can be introduced as almost "canned programs," but the progress
through the year should require more and more ability of the students to
alter parts of the programs, and ultimately to generate their own programs.
   The list of concepts in the body of the report has been trimmed to be

taught plausibly in a one-year course. Topics have been sacrificed from within the customary one-year physics curriculum. These include all aspects of magnetism, inductance, Maxwell's Equations, angular momentum, and special relativity. Some time might be saved *if* chemistry and physics courses are appropriately coordinated, though such cooperation is not natural to university faculties. Similarly, if the mathematics courses can teach complex numbers early, they could be made use of within the physics curriculum for x-ray structure determinations, oscillations, resonance, and stability analysis. Also a major effort must be made to include simple biological examples in the problem sets.

Every attempt should be made to win acceptance of such a new physics course by non-biological majors, in addition to the various possible bio-majors (biology, biochemistry, molecular biology). In an ideal world, a freshman could take either the traditional general physics course or the biology-oriented physics course (B-Physics) as her or his physics requirement. The two courses should be equally challenging and equally based on mathematics, but differ in emphasis. Many majors should be encouraged to accept the B-Physics course as an alternative, including chemistry, math, computer science, and engineering majors. Having several majors accept one course as meeting requirements avoids having students become trapped in a particular major because they have chosen a particular introductory physics course. Also, by giving students flexibility in their curriculum, they will be encouraged to explore opportunities they otherwise might not explore. While a few premeds may appropriately take the B-physics course, its emphasis on physical understandings at the molecular level, and the mathematical sophistication are inappropriate for general premeds. At most universities, an effort to accommodate premeds in the same course would require a substantial dilution of the material presented. While much can be said in favor of redesigning physics courses for premeds, this course is not the appropriate vehicle.

While a conventional laboratory might be adequate, it seems more sensible to consider fundamental changes in laboratory as well as course materials. One possible rationale is based on the usual kind of relationship between course and laboratory physics. A second possible rationale is based on using the laboratory experience to teach principles of engineering as they apply to biology. Sample sets of laboratories for each rationale are sketched in the following two sections. The purpose of the lab would be to reinforce lecture concepts, introduce new concepts particularly suitable to laboratory exploration, illustrate physical principles, and/or experience bio-applications. Error analysis, uncertainty, fluctuations, and noise are probably best treated as part of laboratory experience rather than as topics in physics. Examples from biology should be used when available, and can already start in the section on Newtonian and macroscopic mechanics. Properties of materials (bone, tendon, hair) and biological fluid flows or motions of bacteria or bioparticles in water provide excellent opportunities.

The laboratory should begin with sessions based on step-by-step instruction, data sheets, equations given, and minimal writing. In a later phase, there should be guidelines—laboratories based on *examples* of how to do things, concepts, and a memo report (~1 page). Over the year they should evolve to open-ended questions with minimal reporting (~2 pages). This is a "Crawl, Walk, Run" approach. Students should work as a team consisting of two or three students for all labs. While the work done in lab should be done as a team, all writing assignments should be done by each student to develop writing skills. Whenever possible, students should learn by doing. If students are required to think through the process, they will have a much better understanding of the concepts. It may not be feasible to have a physical lab for all the desired laboratory experiences. Physical laboratories are preferred whenever possible, but both physical and virtual labs should be utilized. LabVIEW and Matlab both offer excellent environments for students to learn laboratory concepts. Web-based learning should also be utilized when particular experiments are not available or may be hard to reproduce locally. Details on the content for such a lab can be found in Chapter 4.

Connections to Engineering in the Biology Curriculum

It is important to bring some ideas from engineering into the education of biology students. The word *function* is used in a similar context in engineering and biology, and *this context does not exist in pure science or mathematics*. Biology, with the impetus to dissect systems to understand their components (top-down), has evolved in the past decade into a molecular science. Now that the human genome is known, and the molecular players of many cell-signaling pathways are identified, biology is turning increasingly to the understanding of complex systems. Understanding function at the systems level requires a way of thinking that is common to many engineers. An engineer takes building blocks to build a system with desired features (bottom-up). Creating (or re-creating) function by building a complex system, and getting it to work, is the ultimate proof that all essential building blocks and how they work in synchrony are truly understood. Getting a system to work typically requires (a) an understanding of the fundamental building blocks, (b) knowledge of the relation between the building blocks, (c) the system's design, or how its components fit together in a productive way, (d) system modeling, (e) construction of the system, and (f) testing the system and its function(s). Understanding cells, organs, and finally animals and plants at the systems level will require that the biologist borrow approaches from engineering, and that engineering principles are introduced early in the education of biologists.

Biology research is really about trying to understand how biology *works*. What actually constitutes such an understanding is often best grappled within an engineering context, where systems have been designed and do work. Students should be frequently confronted throughout their biology curriculum with questions and tasks such as how they would design "xxx," *and how they would test to see whether their conceptual design actually works.* They should be asked to simulate their system, determine its rate constants, determine regimes of stability and instability, investigate regulatory feedback mechanisms, and other challenges. The engineering view has a role in the general biology curriculum, or could be introduced as special-topics biology courses or as specific courses within engineering biomedical engineering/biomaterials programs. Some examples of topics with engineering aspects that might be included within the ordinary biology curriculum can be found in the body of the report. Another appropriate subject is the study of molecules and supramolecular structures from both a biochemical *and a mechanical* perspective. The students should also be thinking of kinetics, rate constants, and other topics addressed in the outline of the physics course. Assuming that biochemistry is already well covered, these concepts with an emphasis on mechanics could be developed in the context of motor proteins, assembly and de-assembly of the cytoskeleton, condensation of DNA, etc. The students could be asked to analyze raw data quantitatively to see the relationship between physical structure, reaction pathways, and function or model the dynamics (e.g., dynamic instabilities) of a system with a given set of parameters.

Seminars

Seminars on research, directed to lower-division undergraduates, can illustrate the relevance of mathematical and computer modeling and analysis. They are effective ways to convey the importance of quantitative and modeling approaches to research in biology. While not directly part of the physics/engineering curriculum for biology, and perhaps best given under the aegis of a biology department, they can have an immense impact on the views of students as to what is of importance.

Many engineering curricula require a capstone design experience, in which students undertake one project that ties together many of the topics they have learned throughout their college career. Borrowing successful models from engineering, a biology capstone course might be required. This course could be a design experience, a research experience, or a combination of the two. The goal should be to give a major experience that requires the students to bring together their diverse knowledge to accomplish the goals of the projects. The students should work as teams under the close guidance of a faculty member. The course should be a one-semester course, although a two-semester sequence is not uncommon in engineering. The teams should be required to accomplish something more than a paper product (i.e., writing a small research proposal should not be sufficient). Instead of research, the students could focus on the development of a biorelated product. In any event, a significant report and presentation should be required. Efforts should be made to have biology students work on multidisciplinary projects with engineering, biomedical engineering, physics, chemistry, and other majors.

The committee brainstormed the following ideas for advanced seminar courses, and some aspects of these courses would also make appropriate capstone projects. They involve bringing together diverse aspects of students' previous education in order to increase their understanding of more complex systems:

- The Mechanics of Organisms as described in Case Study #5 in the body of the committee report.
- Determination of Structure, the chemistry and biology of proteins using methods of diffraction and spectroscopy and including the topics of fluorescence, Fourier transforms, electron spins, and display of 3-D data.
- Biological Imaging including the properties of light, thin lens laws, resolution, and diffraction orders, the lens as a Fourier transform, fluorescence, confocal microscopy, MRI, electron microscopy, tomography, and deconvolution.
- Molecular Biophysics of signal transduction at the cell surface and inside the cell, including the statistics of receptor ligand interactions, life in low Reynolds number, kinases and phosphatases, G-protein coupled cas-

cades, the cytoskeleton and cell adhesion, transcription factors and genetic cascades, and the multiple roles of individual proteins and cross-talk between different pathways (beta catenin for example).

*   Biomedical Systems: a bioengineering/biophysics approach to human physiology. Topics would include organ physiology, hormones and endocrine loops, paracrine effects, systems analysis of control loops, the importance of temporal aspects of hormones, and examples such as cardiac control loops and circadian rhythms.

*   Biological Motors and Molecular Machines.

F

Mathematics and Computer Science Panel Summary

The Mathematics and Computer Science panel was composed of scientists and educators selected for their expertise in mathematics, computer science, or biology, especially knowledge of connections between the fields. The panel met on March 15-16, 2001, at Boston University to discuss how to integrate that kind of knowledge into the undergraduate education of future biomedical researchers.

EXPERTISE OF MEMBERS OF THE PANEL

Nancy Kopell is W.G. Aurelio Professor of Mathematics and Science and co-director of the Center for BioDynamics (a multidisciplinary center for biology, mathematics, and engineering) at Boston University. Her research includes the mathematics of self-organizing systems (both physical and biological); currently she is focusing on dynamics of the nervous system, especially rhythmic activity associated with cognition and motor control. She was awarded a MacArthur Fellowship and is a member of the National Academy of Sciences. She received a bachelor's degree from Cornell University and her PhD from the University of California at Berkeley.

Robert Blystone is professor of biology at Trinity University in San Antonio, Texas. His research is on the nitration of thermally stressed tissue, computer reconstruction of tissue, and educational issues related to quantitative learning in biology. He is a Fellow of the American Association for the Advancement of Science and has been named the Scott Professor for Teaching and the Piper Professor of Texas. He serves on the education committee of the American Society for Cell Biology and the college committee of the National Association of Biology Teachers. He has participated in many conferences, workshops, and panels on education, the most recent being the Mathematics Association of America's study of Mathematics Education Reform in Biology and Chemistry. He teaches courses on Biological Visualization, Developmental Biology, and Organsimal Structure & Function. He received a BS in biological sciences from the University of Texas at El Paso and an MA and PhD in zoology from the University of Texas at Austin.

Louis Gross is director of the Institute for Environmental Modeling and professor of ecology and evolutionary biology and professor of mathematics at the University of Tennessee in Knoxville. His research interests include mathematical ecology, computational ecology, quantitative training for life science students, photosynthetic dynamics, and parallel computation for ecological models. He was the co-director of courses and workshops on mathematical ecology held by the International Centre for Theoretical Physics in Trieste, Italy, between 1986 and 2000. He has organized two NSF-sponsored workshops on quantitative curriculum development for life science students. In 1999 he taught an NSF Chataqua Course entitled Life Science Education: Preparing Fearless Biologists. At Tennessee he teaches courses on Mathematical Ecology, Mathematical Modeling and Evolutionary Theory, and Basic Concepts in Ecology. He received his BS degree from Drexel University and his PhD in Applied Mathematics from Cornell University.

Richard Karp is senior research scientist at the International Computer Science Institute in Berkeley, California, and professor of computer science and adjunct professor of molecular biotechnology at the University of Washington in Seattle. He has done research on NP-completeness, fast parallel algorithms, string matching, and, most recently, computational biology. His current research is on the application of algorithms, combinatorial mathematics, and probability to problems in genomics. He is particularly interested in physical mapping, in the analysis of genome sequencing strategies, and in the application of algorithms to the study of gene expression. He is a member of the National Academy of Sciences and the National Academy of Engineering. He was awarded the Fulkerson Prize in Discrete Mathematics, Lanchester Prize in Operations Research, ACM Turing Award, and the U.S. National Medal of Science. He is a member of the National Advisory Board for Computer Professionals for Social Responsibility. He received a Distinguished Teaching Award from the UC Berkeley Academic Senate. His teaching at the University of Washington includes Algorithms in Molecular Biology. He has bachelor's and PhD degrees from Harvard University.

Eric Lander is director of the Whitehead Institute and professor of biology at the Massachusetts Institute of Technology. His research interests include human, mouse, and population genetics, and computational methods in biology. He was awarded a MacArthur Fellowship and is a Fellow of the American Association for the Advancement of Science. He is a member of the National Academy of Sciences and the Institute of Medicine. He was on the NRC Committee on the Mathematical Sciences in Genome and Protein Structure Research, which produced the report *Calculating the Secrets of Life*. He has taught courses on mathematics, statistics, and economics, and developed new courses on bidding and bargaining, artificial intelligence, and on science-based businesses. He was awarded MIT's Baker Memorial Prize for Excellence in Undergraduate Teaching. He received his bachelor's degree from Princeton University and his PhD in Mathematics from Oxford University.

Markus Meister is professor of molecular and cellular biology at Harvard University. His research is in the field of systems neuroscience, specifically using retina to understand how large systems of neurons represent and process information. He has been a PEW Scholar, NSF Presidential Faculty Fellow, Lucille P. Markey Scholar, Fellow of the Helen Hay Whitney Foundation, and is a member of the *Stiftung Maximilianeum* and the *Studienstifung des Deutschen Volkes* of Germany. He teaches graduate and undergraduate students in the Molecular and Cellular Biology Program; his courses include Experimental Neuroscience and Function of Neural Systems. He received his PhD from the California Institute of Technology.

Alan Perelson is head of the Los Alamos National Laboratory's Theoretical Biology and Biophysics Division. His research interests include mathematical and theoretical biology with an emphasis on problems in immunology and virology. He has taught courses in the biophysics field at UC-Berkeley,

Brown University, and the Ecole Normale Superieure in Paris. He is on the Board of Governors for the Institute of Mathematics and its Applications at the University of Minnesota. He is a member of the Science Board, head of the Theoretical Immunology Program, and an external professor of the Santa Fe Institute. He is a past president of the Society for Mathematical Biology. He was awarded an NIH Research Career Development Award. He serves on the Springer-Verlag editorial board responsible for textbooks in biomathematics. He received his bachelor's degree in life science and electrical engineering from the Massachusetts Institute of Technology and a PhD in biophysics from University of California at Berkeley.

Louise Ryan is professor of biostatistics at Harvard School of Public Health. Her research is on statistical methods related to environmental health research and risk assessment. She is a Fellow of the American Statistical Association and in the International Statistics Institute. She received the Speigelman Award from the American Public Health Association. She is currently a co-editor of *Biometrics* and president of the Eastern North American Region of the International Biometric Society. She has served on advisory boards for several government agencies, including the National Toxicology Program and the Environmental Protection Agency, as well as NRC committees on toxicological effects of mercury and arsenic in drinking water. She teaches graduate courses at the Harvard School of Public Health and is the program director for an Initiative for Minority Student Development Grant, which supports summer internships and predoctoral training. In addition, she is the director of the Summer Program in Biostatistics at Harvard School of Public Health, which targets undergraduate math majors from underrepresented minority groups. She received the Harvard School of Public Health Mentoring Award in 2000. She received her PhD from Harvard University.

DeWitt Sumners is the Robert O. Lawton Distinguished Professor of Mathematics at Florida State University and co-director of the Program in Mathematics and Molecular Biology. His current research projects include DNA topology and analyzing the function of the human brain. He specializes in knot theory and applications of topology to molecular biology and polymer configuration, both in theory development and computational simulation. He serves on the NRC Board on Mathematical Sciences and was on the Committee on Mathematical Challenges from Computational Chemistry. He teaches undergraduates at Florida State, including introductory calculus courses. He has presented to Congress on Calculating the Secrets of Life: Mathematics and Medicine. He received his bachelor's degree in physics from Louisiana State University and PhD in mathematics from the University of Cambridge.

Consultant to the committee:

Charles Peskin is professor of mathematics at the Courant Institute of Mathematical Sciences, New York University. He has done extensive mathematical and numerical analysis of physiological problems, particularly in cardiac fluid dynamics and the study of the heart's architecture. His research interests include the application of mathematics and computing to problems arising in medicine and biology, fluid dynamics of the heart, and molecular machinery within biological cells. He is a winner of the NYU Alumni Association's Great Teacher Award, a MacArthur Fellowship, the James H. Wilkinson Prize in Numerical Analysis and Scientific Computing, and the New York City Mayor's Award for Excellence in Science and Technology. He teaches a freshman honors seminar in computer simulation. He received his bachelor's degree in engineering and applied physics from Harvard University and his PhD in physiology from Yeshiva University.

REPORT OF THE MATHEMATICS AND COMPUTER SCIENCE PANEL

It was the unanimous view of the mathematics and computer science panels that there need to be major revisions in the education of scientists working on cutting-edge biology questions. Biology is changing from a purely experimental science done at the bench to one in which large databases of information and quantitative models play a significant role in the day-to-day life of a research biologist. As the role of the 30,000 or so genes in the human begin to unfold, new means will be needed to understand the interactions between gene products that lead to the coordinated activities of the cell. Gene networks, metabolic networks, neural networks, and cell signaling are all terms bantered about and reflect the need for biologists to view and understand the coordinated activities of large numbers of components of the complex systems underlying life. While today's students learn about the importance of in vitro models, students in 2010 should be prepared for doing in silico (or computer) experiments, which may be as commonplace as today's in vitro experimental systems. To prepare for this sea change in activities, undergraduate biology majors who plan to pursue a research career need to be educated in a more quantitative manner. The panel felt that no one curriculum should be mandated because students interested in different areas of biology could benefit from different courses, even at the undergraduate level. Furthermore, it made a distinction between the "quantitative biologist," who works at the interface of math/computer science and biology, and the "research biologist," who needs familiarity with a range of mathematical and computational ideas without necessarily being expert. Thus, the panel felt that flexibility in offerings is more advisable than a fixed curriculum.

The panel suggested that all biology majors, not just future biomedical researchers, should be exposed to and develop a conceptual understanding for the idea of rate of change, modeling, equilibria and stability, structure of a system, interactions among components, data and measurement, stochasticity, visualizing, and algorithms. More details on these concepts are in Chapter 2. In addition, future biomedical researchers should graduate with the ability to do in-depth analysis in a subset of the listed topics. In addition to these content recommendations, the panel recommended early exposure to quantitative ideas, via a reorganization of the first-year biology course to introduce a variety of quantitative concepts in the context of biological themes. A similar approach for upper-level students would integrate quantitative ideas into courses such as genomics, ecology, and neurobiology. One mechanism for doing this is to offer a standard course in a "quantitatively intensive" version, analogous to the "writing intensive" courses offered by some schools. The quantitatively intensive version would involve more credit hours and could be taught by a different faculty member as a seminar or a laboratory. The panel also recommended that research opportunities in quantitative biology be encouraged and funded.

The panel recommended curricular changes beyond the biology department. Many biology majors would benefit from new courses in the department of mathematics. The panel proposed a new sequence designed to condense many of the existing undergraduate mathematics courses into three or four semesters. Computer science courses designed for biology students would also be beneficial. Changes in the curriculum will not be enough to produce the desired cohort of quantitatively trained biologists; it will also be necessary to help train the teachers of these future scientists, and to provide both the teachers and the students with appropriate teaching materials. This will require funding to produce, publicize, and/or adapt this material.

The panel felt that students interested in biology are opting to major in other disciplines because they do not feel quantitatively challenged in the traditional biology courses. They would like to attract these students by offering a quantitative track within the biology major. In a track designed for a quantitative biologist, a student might take one year of standard calculus, which many students now take in high school; one semester of linear algebra; one semester of statistics; a one-semester course on ordinary differential equations that includes some numerical work, possibly with packages such as Matlab; and one course on discrete mathematics tailored toward genome problems. These courses could be standard math classes and thus not add a burden on the biology department, although the discrete mathematics course could be of the type listed below for research biologists. Such a track can be flexibly designed for students with different educational goals. Some students may wish to pursue a career in biology that involves the development and analysis of models, databases, etc. Such students would require more education in math, computer science, and physical science than the wet-lab biologist who needs to be familiar with quantitative reasoning but who will not be creating new quantitative tools and analyses. Clearly, it is a difficult task to identify the needs of students in the earliest days of their entry into the study of biology, but if appropriate choices are available, students will self-select the track that fits their capabilities and interests.

In a track for research biologists, new courses are needed. The level of mathematics in this track would not be as great as for the quantitative biologist. However, more emphasis would need to be placed on motivating mathematics and statistics and showing how they are used. Rather than doing standard calculus, linear algebra, and differential equations, a one-year course on mathematics for biologists should be designed. This course should be based on biological examples and include methods of solving problems, but with more emphasis on standard packages, e.g. Matlab and Mathematica, than a course for mathematics majors or quantitative biologists. In addition, a second course (one semester or a year) encompassing ideas of genomics, bioinformatics, statistics and probability, discrete mathematics, the use of databases, tools for searching databases, and some introduction to programming or writing scripts should be implemented.

Students in either track would benefit from the opportunity to do basic research. The National Science Foundation Division of Mathematical Sciences (NSF DMS) funds a collection of REU (Research Experiences for Undergraduates) summer programs each year. Each program has 10-15 students in residence at a university for six weeks or so of intensive mathematics; the students individually and collectively attack mathematics research problems. It would be possible to run REU programs in mathematics departments that were geared for biology undergraduates with the cooperation of the local university biology department and wet laboratory access. One scenario would be for the students to take a math-modeling course and learn to use canned software packages of interest in modern biology in the morning, and work in a wet biology lab in the afternoon. Ideally, the mathematics, calculation, and visualization techniques they learn in the math department would be applicable toward the analysis of the data they would be generating in the wet lab. Perhaps the funding for such biologically oriented REU summer programs would come jointly from the mathematics and biology directorates at the NSF (and perhaps the NIH).

Interdisciplinary Modeling Courses

The panel advocated the teaching of interdisciplinary courses in modeling, both at the introductory level and the advanced level. Interdisciplinary courses are distinguished by several characteristics. First, they are intended for a mixed audience that covers a spectrum from students who think of themselves as primarily biological to students who think of themselves as primarily mathematical or computational (and including, of course, students who already think of themselves as primarily interdisciplinary). Having students with different majors enrolled in the same course is an asset. It encourages discussion across traditional disciplinary boundaries and it is useful for students to see familiar material in an unfamiliar light. This will happen in such a course across the whole spectrum of students, although different aspects of the course will be familiar/unfamiliar to different students. Students with different backgrounds will be able to help each other with different aspects of the course material. The panel felt that it was often advantageous to organize interdisciplinary courses around the biological material. Mathematical/computational methods should be taught, but on a need-to-know basis. The emphasis should not be on the methods per se, but rather on how the methods elucidate the biology. The goal should be to see biology in a whole new light as a result of the mathematical/computational approach to the subject. Interdisciplinary courses can be taught either by individuals or by interdisciplinary teams. The people who teach such courses should, either individually or collectively, have actual experience in the application of mathematics or computation to biological problems. If team teaching is used, great care must be taken to avoid fragmentation of the course into separate modules on biology, mathematics, and computation. The point of the course should be to bring the mathematics and computation to bear on the biology.

Where in the undergraduate curriculum should interdisciplinary courses appear? Ideally, they should appear in both the first and last year of the curriculum. The purpose of the first-year course would be to provide strong motivation by showing how useful mathematics and computing can be in biology. The student thus motivated would then go on to learn more mathematics and computing, as well as biology, in the middle years of the curriculum. The interdisciplinary course in the last year would then put all that knowledge to work in an integrated way. The first-year course is more difficult to design because of the limited knowledge of the student. One possible format is a "whet the appetite" course that could be given to a relatively large class of freshmen. The goal would not be to provide in-depth, hands-on experience, but rather to expose students to the broad range of interesting work that can be done at the interface of biology and mathematics. A series of speakers would present case studies on a wide range of topics such as various aspects of genomics, environmental science, medical statistics, computational biology, mathematical biology, toxicology, or risk assessment. The twin purposes of such a course would be for biology students to see that mathematics and computation can play an important role in their work, and for mathematics and computer science students to see the potential for applying quantitative methods (statistics, applied mathematics, computer science) to biology and medicine. Because not all schools would have faculty with the expertise to run such a course, they might need to rely on a series of outside visitors. In any case, it would probably run more like a colloquium series than an actual course.

At the opposite extreme, a second possible format is the first-year seminar. This seminar could be devised so that students do hands-on computer simulations of biological phenomena. Such a course would meet alternately in a classroom and a computer laboratory. Class time would be devoted to the exposition of mathematical models in biology, and of methods for studying the behavior of such models by computer. The computer lab would be a hands-on experience in which students work individually or in small groups on computing projects. Each research team would report on its work to the class as a whole. Suitable topics at this level may be drawn from physiology (blood circulation, gas exchange in the lung, control of cell volume, electrical activity of neurons, renal countercurrent mechanism, muscle mechanics) or population biology (epidemic and endemic disease, ecological dynamics, population genetics, evolution). Mathematical models would either involve systems of algebraic equations (accessible with high school mathematics) or ordinary differential equations (made tractable and understandable via Euler's method without any formal course in differential equations required). Simulations involving random numbers can also be done with only an intuitive introduction to probability and the use of a random number generator. A computer language such as Matlab makes it easy to write programs that implement Euler's method (and other similar methods), and also provides easy access to graphical output, including animations. Black-box software that solves differential equations should be avoided because it short-changes the educational value of seeing how the problem is actually being solved.

The senior-level interdisciplinary course could reprise many of the same topics at a different level of sophistication. Where the first-year course might have considered only point neurons, for example, the senior course might consider spatially distributed neurons, thus moving up mathematically from ordinary to partial differential equations. Again, numerical methods provide a path to understanding without a formal course in partial differential equations. Besides the use of more advanced methods, the senior-level course should be characterized by a greater emphasis on original research projects conducted by the students. The projects in this course would be similar to senior theses, but would be done at least in some cases by teams of students, and in all cases in the context of a group of like-minded students, engaged in similar interdisciplinary efforts, to whom the work would eventually be reported.

Competency and Expertise in Computer Science

The panel recommended that all biology students receive instruction in computer science. It is useful to distinguish three levels of aspiration concerning the role of computer science in undergraduate biology education.

Fluency with Information Technology

The goal is to prepare biology students to use information technology today and to adapt to changes in information technology in the future.

They should acquire an understanding of how computers work, basic programming skills, and fluency in using networks and databases. A course at this level should include simple programming assignments. To give it a biological accent, there should be laboratory experiences using Medline, Genbank, and other biological databases, as well as physiological and ecological simulations. One assignment might ask students to use computer searches to track down all known information about a given gene and the protein it encodes, including both structure and function. This would involve exploring the internal structure of the gene (exons, introns, promoter, transcription factor binding sites); the regulatory control of the gene; sequence homologs of the gene and the protein; the structure and function of the protein; gene interaction networks and metabolic pathways involving the protein; and interactions of the protein with other proteins and with small molecules.

The NRC report *Being Fluent with Information Technology* lays out the structure and objectives of such a course in detail, but is not oriented specifically toward biologists.

Capability in Program Design for Computational Biology and Genomics Applications

A course at this level provides the minimal skills required to be an effective computer user within a computationally oriented biology research team. A good example is a course by Adam Arkin at Berkeley. His course introduces students to structured software development and selected principles of computer science, with applications in computational biology and allied disciplines. The principal language used for instruction is Java, with a course module on Perl. Examples and tutorials are drawn from problems in computational biology. The course requires one significant programming project, preferably biologically oriented.

Capability in Developing Software Tools for Use by the Biology Community

A foundation for reaching this level is provided by courses in discrete mathematics, data structures, and algorithms. According to the student's interests, these could be followed by courses in database management systems, information systems, software engineering, computer graphics, or computer simulation techniques. Biologists could select courses that teach the design and specification of database and information systems, not merely their internal structure.

Graph theory and combinatorics are at the heart of many of the successful applications of mathematics and computer science in high-throughput genomics research (microarray chips) and rational drug design; the panel believes that this interface will continue to grow in importance. Computational geometry and the ability to describe, visualize, and computationally compare complicated surfaces in space will become an important area in proteomics and computational medicine.

Teaching Materials and Faculty Development

Standard texts either need to be revised or replaced by more quantitative texts. The texts for most courses in elementary discrete mathematics are not especially exciting. They are filled with definitions but do not challenge the students with interesting problems. More exciting courses are taught by Stephen Rudich at Carnegie-Mellon and by Alistair Sinclair and Umesh Vazirani at Berkeley (CS 70). Terry Speed at Berkeley has developed an introductory statistics course in which the motivating examples are drawn from genomics.

It should be possible to develop courses in discrete mathematics, probability, and algorithms that emphasize applications in biology. It is particularly easy to find motivating examples from genomics and genetics, since those subjects are inherently combinatorial and probabilistic. As one example, sequence alignment is an ideal vehicle for introducing dynamic programming. Graph theory can be linked to sequencing by hybridization. Pedigree analysis and the design of genetic crosses abound with combinatorial puzzles. Probability can be illustrated through the analysis of sequencing and mapping strategies or pooling designs. Fred Roberts at Rutgers has done excellent work in this area (*The Scientist* 9[14], July 10, 1995).

There are not many programs designed specifically to impart quantitative literacy to biology faculty. Some existing programs target other audiences, such as quantitative training of K-12 students, high school teachers, predoctoral students, and postdoctoral students. Joe Rosenstein at Rutgers and Maria Klawe at the University of British Columbia are very active in developing such programs. In addition, The Keck Center in Houston, with sponsorship from NSF and NLM, runs a computational biology training program for predoctoral and postdoctoral fellows. A summer short course might be an appropriate vehicle for enhancing the quantitative literacy of undergraduate biology faculty; NSF sponsors such short courses in other fields. The computer science component of the program might be modeled after Adam Arkin's programming course described above. Terry Speed's statistics course (also described above) might be a model for the statistics component.

G

Workshop on Innovative
Undergraduate Biology Education

Silvertree Hotel, Snowmass Village, Colorado
August 12-14, 2001

EXPERTISE OF WORKSHOP PARTICIPANTS

Julian Adams is a professor of biology at the University of Michigan, in Ann Arbor. His research is on evolution of microorganisms and population genetics in microorganisms and humans. He has held visiting appointments at universities in Brazil and Germany. In 1996 he received a Faculty Recognition Award from Michigan and was appointed chair of its Department of Biology. He serves as associate editor for the journals *Molecular Biology and Evolution* and *Genetica* and was chair of the 1997 Gordon Research Conference on Microbial Population Biology. At Michigan, he has been involved in the development of the university's Life Sciences Initiative. He received his PhD degree from the University of California at Davis.

Ann Burgess is a distinguished senior lecturer at the University of Wisconsin-Madison and the director of the Biology Core Curriculum, a four-semester intercollege honors program that provides students with a broad, rigorous introduction to biology and allows them subsequently to specialize in any field of biological science. She teaches the first two laboratory courses in the sequence and has a particular interest in laboratory projects that involve undergraduates in the process of science, including effectively communicating their ideas with peers. She worked with the faculty team that teaches the final semester of the sequence to change it from a lecture-based course to one based on cooperative learning. She is active in several UW-Madison and national efforts to improve science education, including the BioQUEST Consortium and the National Institute for Science Education's College Level One team.

A. Malcolm Campbell is an associate professor of biology at Davidson College in North Carolina. He recently completed a sabbatical position at the Institute for Systems Biology in Seattle. He is the founder and director of the Genome Consortium for Active Teaching and is the author of *Discovering Genomics, Proteomics and Bioinformatics*, the first genomics textbook. He is also the co-editor in chief of the journal *Cell Biology Education.*

Denice Denton is dean of the College of Engineering and a professor of electrical engineering at the University of Washington in Seattle. She was co-director of the NSF National Institute for Science Education at the University of Wisconsin-Madison for the 1995-1996 academic year. She has taught a course called Ways of Knowing, designed to provide first-year students with a learning experience in a small class environment.

Mike Doyle is vice president of Research Corporation and professor of chemistry at the University of Arizona. He has also been a member of the faculty at Hope College in Holland, Michigan, and at Trinity University in San Antonio, Texas. He has been active with ACS, the Council on Undergraduate Research, and the National Conferences on Undergraduate Research. He has served on several NSF panels on undergraduate education and research and NRC committees on undergraduate science education and career paths for graduates in the physical sciences and mathematics. He is the recipient of numerous awards for research and education, including the George C. Pimentel Award for Chemical Education.

Billy Joe Evans is a professor of chemistry at the University of Michigan in Ann Arbor. He received the Presidential Awards for Excellence in Science, Mathematics and Engineering Mentoring for his work on undergraduate and graduate programs to enhance minority participation in science. Evans received the Catalyst Award for Excellence in College Chemistry Teaching from the Chemical Manufacturers Association and the American Chemical Society National Award for encouraging disadvantaged youth to pursue careers in the chemical sciences. He also serves on the Committee on Professional Training of the American Chemical Society.

Lou Gross is director of the Institute for Environmental Modeling and professor of ecology and evolutionary biology and professor of mathematics at the University of Tennessee in Knoxville. He has organized two NSF-sponsored workshops on quantitative curriculum development for life science students. In 1999 he taught an NSF Chautauqua Course entitled Life Science Education: Preparing Fearless Biologists. At Tennessee he teaches courses on Mathematical Ecology, Mathematical Modeling and Evolutionary Theory, and Basic Concepts in Ecology.

Keith Howard is an associate professor of biology at Morehouse College in Atlanta, Georgia. He received his PhD in plant pathology from Ohio State University. He teaches laboratories and lectures in plant biology and is active in Project Kaleidoscope.

John Jungck is Mead Chair of the Sciences and professor of biology at Beloit College. He is a Fellow of the American Association for the Advancement of Science, a Fulbright Professor to Thailand, and a member of NRC's Committee on Undergraduate Science Education (2002-2005). He is PI and co-founder of the BioQUEST Curriculum Consortium. Over the past 16 years, he and his colleagues at other institutions have been leading the effort to build *The BioQUEST Library*, a collection of computer-based tools, simulations, databases, and textual materials that support collaborative, open-ended investigations in biology. He is chair of the education committee of the Society for Mathematical Biology, serves on the education committee of the American Institute for Biological Sciences, and is on the editorial board of *Cell Biology Education*, which is published by the American Society of Cell Biologists. His research is in mathematical molecular evolution and computational biology (bioinformatics), and their application to teaching and learning biology.

Priscilla Laws is professor of physics at Dickinson College, in Carlisle, Pennsylvania. As part of the Workshop Physics Project that she initiated in 1986, she has developed curricular materials, apparatus, and computer-based software and hardware for students at the high school and college levels. She has received awards for software design and curriculum innovation in the sciences from many organizations. She recently directed a major NSF-funded project that involves PIs at five institutions in a quest to promote activity-based physics teaching.

Jerry R. Mohrig is Herman and Gertrude Mosier Stark Professor in the Natural Sciences and professor of chemistry at Carleton College in Northfield, Minnesota. Actively involved in science education reform for many years, he has served leadership roles with the American Chemical Society, Project Kaleidoscope, and Council on Undergraduate Research. Jerry has co-authored two textbooks, *Experimental Organic Chemistry* and *Chemistry in Perspective*, in addition to many articles on organic chemistry and chemical education. He has been recognized for excellence in the teaching of chemistry by the James Flack Norris Award of the American Chemical Society and the Catalyst Award of the Chemical Manufacturers Association.

Jeanne Narum is the founding director of Project Kaleidoscope (PKAL), an informal national alliance taking a leadership role in efforts to strengthen learning of undergraduates in the fields of science, mathematics, and engineering. Through a coordinated series of workshops, national meetings, and print and electronic publications, PKAL presents the work of individuals and institutions having positive impact in attracting students into the study of STEM fields and in motivating them to persist and succeed. The intent of PKAL activities is to encourage the widespread adaptation of such programs that work and support those taking the lead in reform. Nearly 800 colleges and universities have been involved in PKAL since its beginning in 1989. Narum is the project director for PKAL grants from the National Science Foundation (EHR/DUE), FIPSE (U.S. Department of Education), the Exxon Mobil Foundation, and the W.M. Keck Foundation.

Fred Rudolph is Ralph and Dorothy Looney Professor and chair of the Department of Biochemistry and Cell Biology at Rice University. He also serves as executive director of the Institute of Biosciences and Bioengineering at Rice. He has developed a number of educational initiatives particularly in the K-12 area and in undergraduate and graduate curriculum reform. He has been program director for grants from the Howard Hughes Medical Institute for undergraduate biological science initiatives and various educational grants from NSF and NIH and from other foundations.

Patricia Soochan received bachelor and master of science degrees from George Washington University in 1977 and 1981. In 1994 she joined the undergraduate science education program at the Howard Hughes Medical Institute, where she is now a program officer engaged in all aspects of competition and award management from system design to policy development. In 1982 she became a biochemist at Bethesda Research Labs, later to be known as Life Technologies. Her work included conducting biotechnology workshops in France and Brazil. In 1987 she became a senior information specialist at Social and Scientific Systems, a consultant to the National Cancer Institute. There she worked with physicians in preparing reports of investigational cancer therapies. In 1991 she joined the National Science Foundation as a science assistant/biologist involved in grants management in the cell biology program.

Millard Susman is a professor emeritus in the Laboratory of Genetics at the Medical School and College of Agricultural and Life Sciences of the University of Wisconsin-Madison and continues to serve as the unofficial director of UW's Center for Biology Education, a campus-wide organization dedicated to the innovation and enhancement of biology education in years K-16 and beyond. He is one of the founders of UW's BioCore curriculum and is active in the development of new teaching materials, both print and computer-based. He serves on numerous university committees and is currently working on a project with the NRC to create a summer institute for undergraduate biology education.

Sheldon Wettack is vice president and dean of faculty and professor of chemistry at Harvey Mudd College in Claremont, California. His initial academic appointment was in the chemistry department at Hope College, where he mentored about 30 undergraduates with support from a variety of individual research grants. His administrative work began when he was appointed dean for the natural sciences at Hope. He has served at the University of Richmond as arts and sciences dean and as president of Wabash College. He moved to Harvey Mudd in 1993. He is currently the project director of Harvey Mudd's NSF-AIRE grant and of the Claremont Colleges' technology grant from the Mellon Foundation.

AGENDA OF THE WORKSHOP

Workshop on Innovative Undergraduate Biology Education
Silvertree Hotel, Snowmass Village, Colorado
August 12-14, 2001

Sunday, August 12

6:45 pm   *Welcome and Overview of Bio2010*
                 Lubert Stryer

8:00 pm   *Goals of the Workshop*
                 Sharon Long

Monday, August 13

8:30 am   *Interdisciplinary Courses and Labs, Session I*
                 Denice Denton and Keith Howard (Chairs)

                 Quantitative Life Sciences Education: Some Lessons
                 from a Ten-year Effort
                 Lou Gross

                 Workshop Physics
                 Priscilla Laws

                 Interdisciplinary Labs
                 Sheldon Wettack

                 BioQUEST Curriculum Consortium
                 John Jungck

11:00 am   *Challenges of Interdisciplinary Education*
                 Jim Gentile

1:00 pm   *Interdisciplinary Courses and Labs, Session II*
                 Fred Rudolph and Billy Joe Evans (Chairs)

ChemLinks
Jerry Mohrig

BioCore
Ann Burgess

Undergraduate Research Project: Life Sciences Initiative
Julian Adams

GCAT: Genomics Consortium for Active Teaching
Malcolm Campbell

Symbiosis: An Interdisciplinary Science Seminar
Millard Susman

7:00 pm   Dinner, followed by Discussion of Topics
Seating by Assigned Discussion Groups

Topic 1: Interdisciplinary Courses and Labs
Led by Jeanne Narum

Topic 2: Research Experiences and Independent Projects
Led by Mike Doyle

Topic 3: The Web and Other Shared Resources
Led by Patricia Soochan

Tuesday, August 14

9:00 am   *Presentation and Discussion of Reports from the Dinner Groups*
Led by Jeanne Narum, Mike Doyle, and Patricia Soochan

11:00 am   *Group Writing of Workshop Findings and Recommendations*
Led by Sharon Long and Jim Gentile

1:45 pm   Adjournment

Index